Rivers and Streams

PATRICIA A. FINK MARTIN

FRANKLIN WATTS
A Division of Grolier Publishing
New York   London   Hong Kong   Sydney
Danbury, Connecticut

To my family

Note to Readers: Terms defined in glossary are bold in the text. In most cases, measurements are given in both metric and English units. Wherever measurements are given in only one system, the units provided are the most appropriate for that situation.

Photographs ©: AP/Wide World Photos: 106 (Mike Okoniewski); ENP Images: cover (Alan Kearney); Photo Researchers: 89 (Treat Davidson/National Audubon Society), 70 (Leonard Lee Rue III), 52 (Walker); Rob Simpson Nature Stock: 84 (Rob & Ann Simpson), 58; Tom Stack & Associates: 44 (David M. Dennis); Visuals Unlimited: 43 (Brokaw Photography), 11 (J. D. Cunningham), 56 (Maslowski), 69 (Joe McDonald), 61 (G. L. Twiest), 79.Illustrations by Bob Italiano and Steve Savage
Book interior design and pagination by Carole Desnoes

Library of Congress Cataloging-in-Publication Data

Martin, Patricia A. Fink, 1955–
   Rivers and Streams / Patricia A. Fink Martin.
     p. cm. — (Exploring ecosystems)
   Includes bibliographical references and index.
   Summary: Provides instructions for projects and activities that explore rivers and stream habitats and explains why these environments should be preserved and protected.
   ISBN 0-531-11523-2 (lib. bdg.)   0-531-15969-8 (pbk.)
   1. Stream ecology—Study and teaching—Activity programs—Juvenile literature. [1. Stream ecology—Experiments. 2. Rivers—Experiments. 3. Ecology Experiments. 4. Experiments.]
I. Title. II. Series.
QH541.5.S7M375 1999
577.6'4'0712—dc21   98-10117
                                 CIP
                                 AC

GROLIER
PUBLISHING 1 2 3 4 5 6 7 8 9 10 R 08 07 06 05 04 03 02 01 00 99

Acknowledgments

Special thanks to the following people for their insights and suggestions: Lloyd Swift and Wayne Swank of Coweeta Hydrologic Laboratory; Wayne Minshall and his students at the Stream Ecology Center, Idaho State University; Ken Cummins and Al Steinman at the South Florida Water Management District; Steve Vandas of the United States Geological Survey; and everyone at Seminole County Community College.

Contents

Introduction

IT'S ALWAYS MOVING BUT IT NEVER goes anywhere. It can blast holes in solid stone and carve through massive layers of rock. It moves huge boulders, trees, and even houses. Much of the surface of Earth has been shaped and sculpted by its movement.

What is the force that accomplishes these feats? The moving water of rivers and streams. From the thundering majesty of Niagara Falls to the crashing, turbulent Colorado River, we are drawn to the power and excitement of running water. But even a small neighborhood creek can be a fascinating place to explore. The never-ending flow of water captures our attention. Where did this water come from? How did it get here? Where is it going?

Whether it's the mighty Mississippi or a trickling mountain brook, all rivers and streams consist of water that is not reabsorbed by the soil. Most **channels** of water cut across Earth's surface, seeking the path of least resistance, but some rivers and streams run underground for part of

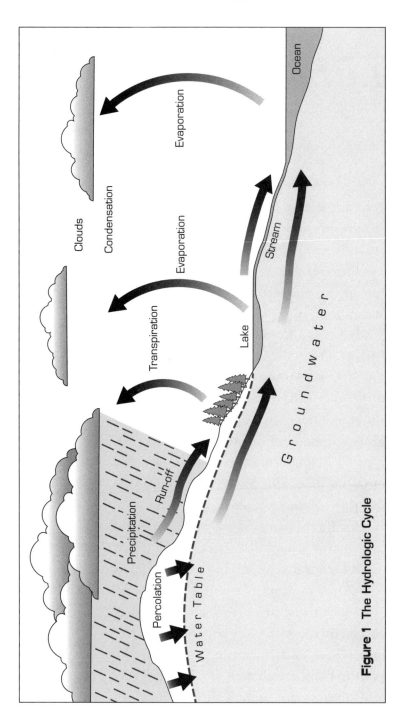

Figure 1 The Hydrologic Cycle

their journey. Regardless, the water flows on, joining other streams and rivers on its way to the sea.

The ocean is both the end and the beginning of water's endless journey. Through the cycle of **evaporation** and **precipitation,** water falls on land in the form of rain or snow and returns to the ocean by way of mountain brooks, creeks, streams, and rivers (see Figure 1).

We use many terms to describe bodies of running water, including **arroyo,** kill, **run,** and reach. Spring runs begin where water seeps from the ground, usually in a slow trickle. A river is a larger body of flowing water that usually receives several **tributaries** along its route.

Because these terms lack precise meanings, scientists use a classification system to rank, or order, streams according to the way their channels link up along the journey from the **source** to the ocean. Small streams that carry water from a source such as a spring don't usually flow directly into the ocean. Instead, they flow into other streams which, in turn, combine to form larger streams. These larger streams unite to form rivers, which eventually lead to the ocean.

Keeping Streams in Order

This chain or network of streams and rivers can be classified according to **stream order.** The streams at the beginning of the system are called first-order streams. With no tributaries, first-order streams receive water directly from a source such as a spring, a lake, melting snow, rainwater, or even a melting glacier. These streams include the narrow cascading waters of steep mountain brooks and the cool, clear water of springs.

As the water continues its journey, these small first-order streams flow into other such streams, and form second-order channels. Second-order streams combine to form larger third-order streams. Two third-order streams join to form a fourth-order stream (see Figure 2 on the next page).

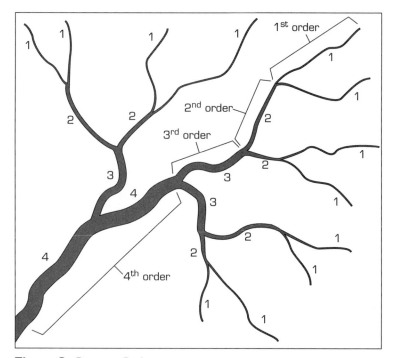

Figure 2 Stream Order

What do these streams look like? Imagine a trout fisherman knee-deep in the water. Against the sound of running water, you hear the swish of the line as she casts, and the soft splash of the lure as it strikes the surface. You have probably just pictured a third- or fourth-order stream.

By the time a stream reaches the seventh order, the channel is wide and deep, and the water is heavy with mud and **silt.** These large streams are rivers. Streams rarely reach the tenth order before flowing into the ocean. The Mississippi River is the only example of a tenth-order stream in North America—some people even classify it as a thirteenth-order stream!

Running waters can also be classified according to the frequency of water flow. Permanent or **perennial streams** flow all year round. **Intermittent streams** flow only during the wet season or after a period of heavy

Common in dry areas of the West, arroyos can fill with treacherous, fast-flowing water without warning.

rain. At other times, these intermittent streams are just dry streambeds. Even more short-lived are the **ephemeral streams** found in very dry areas of the western United States. These streams flow in deep ravines or arroyos only during intense rainfall.

But a stream or river is more than just a body of flowing water. It includes the plants and animals that live in and around it, the nutrients dissolved in its water, and the soil and rocks carried in its flow. Even the dead leaves and branches that drop into the water are important parts of that stream. This unique body of water, with its living and nonliving components, constitutes an **ecosystem.**

This book will help you explore the ecosystems of rivers and streams. Choose from dozens of exciting activities: Learn how to monitor a local stream for pollution; make a map of a shallow stream; and pan for gold. See how rivers erode the land by building a model; set up an aquarium for a water strider and amaze your friends with an insect that walks on water. Whether you're an armchair explorer or enjoy getting your feet wet, this book can take you on many exciting adventures in the world of rivers and streams.

Safety First

Sloshing around in the neighborhood creek looking for stream creatures can be fun. But water, especially running water, can be dangerous. To keep your adventures happy, follow these water safety rules as you try the activities in this book.

1. Always try to explore with a friend. If you do go alone, tell someone where you are going and when you plan to be back.
2. Never step into a stream without first checking its depth and flow. Currents can be deceptively strong and the water might be deeper than it looks.
3. Beware of slippery rocks. In shallow, fast-moving streams, algae growing on the surface of rocks produce a slimy covering that can be slippery.
4. Never wade in water that is deeper than knee-level.
5. Use a wading staff or hiking stick to help you keep your balance.
6. Wear boots or waders in the water. You can use old sneakers as creek shoes if the soles aren't too smooth. Try gluing a piece of indoor-outdoor carpeting to the soles with a waterproof adhesive to give your shoes better traction.
7. Stay away from streams during—and up to a day after—heavy storms. **Flash floods** happen rapidly and often without warning.
8. Watch out for broken glass and rusty metal on the streambed and banks.
9. Beware of poisonous plants or snakes along the bank and in the water.
10. When you collect plants, animals, and water samples, wear gloves and keep your hands away from your face and eyes. Some streams harbor harmful bacteria and other disease-causing microorganisms. Above all, don't drink the water!

Keeping Track

Keeping a journal of your experiences is easy and can be rewarding. All you need is a bound notebook and a waterproof pen or pencil. Keep your journal dry by storing it in a large resealable plastic bag. You may want to purchase a notebook made of water-resistant paper. They are available from certain suppliers (see Appendix).

While you are exploring, record your observations and questions in your journal. Don't assume you can remember everything until you get home! It's easy to forget the details, so write them down while they're fresh in your mind. And, even if you think you can't draw, include sketches of what you see.

You might want to include some of the following data in your journal:

- date, time, location;
- weather conditions (temperature, wind direction and speed, relative humidity, cloud conditions);
- plant-life observations (types, numbers, descriptions);
- animal-life observations (types, numbers, distribution, behaviors, adaptations);
- surrounding area (land-use patterns, special features, odors);
- soil conditions (water saturation, soil type, erosion);
- anything that seemed special or unusual.

While your field journal is your most important piece of equipment, some of the activities in this book call for other kinds of equipment. You will find directions for constructing these devices in the Appendix.

Become the local expert on a shallow stream in your area. If you are conscientious and consistent, your journal will be a valuable record of conditions in that stream over time.

CHAPTER 1

River Cutters and Stream Sculptors: Shaping the Land

SIT BESIDE A MOUNTAIN BROOK AND listen to the soothing sounds of rushing water. Stare into the depths of a dark pool. Have you ever wondered what you would hear below the water's surface? If you took an underwater plunge, you might hear a very unusual symphony of sounds.

Grains of sand grind against one another as the stream lifts them up and bashes them against the pebbles and larger stones. Small pebbles add a sharp *chink chink* to the symphony as they skip and roll along the streambed. At times a loud boom echoes through the water: A large stone, swept up with the current, lands heavily against some rocks.

These are the sounds of a stream at work. Geologists refer to these stream activities as **erosion,** transport, and **deposition.** In the process of erosion, running water picks up pieces of the land over which it travels. Fast-moving water can carry pebbles, large stones, and even boulders, while slower streams carry mostly silt and sand. Deposition occurs when running water encounters something that slows its flow and causes the particles to drop from the water to the streambed.

The driving force behind these activities is the flow of water as it is pulled downhill by **gravity.** That flow is known as the current. The speed at which water moves is the **current velocity.** The geological processes of erosion, transport, and deposition, the physical nature of the streambed, and the stream inhabitants, are all influenced by the current velocity. It is a principal feature of rivers and streams.

Try the activities in this chapter to learn more about the ways in which current velocity affects rivers and streams and shapes Earth's surface.

INVESTIGATION 1

Stream Walk

Are you ready to get your feet wet? Grab your footgear and head for the nearest creek. ***Before you go, review the water safety rules in the Introduction.***

Take a 10-minute stroll upstream and observe the flowing water as you walk. Is the stream channel the same depth all along the stretch? Does the water move at the same speed along that length? Are there any fallen trees, boulders, or other obstructions in the stream?

As water flows through the channel, it slows down or speeds up, it gets shallower or becomes deeper. These changes create a mosaic of habitats, including **riffles,** pools, runs, and **backwaters.** As you walk back downstream, try to locate these habitats.

Regions of shallow, ripply water are called riffles. Here the water moves swiftly over a rock-strewn bed. Riffles often alternate with pools—areas of deeper water. In these deeper regions, the water surface is smooth and the water moves slowly. The streambed is covered with soft material, such as silt, sand, or mud.

You may see deep stretches of fast-moving water. These areas are called runs. Here the water surface may be choppy and the streambed may be rocky. In its downhill rush, water often meets obstacles that divert its flow. Fallen trees or large rocks can produce sheltered areas or backwaters along the bank.

In your journal, sketch the section of stream you have just walked through and mark the stream habitats you found.

PROJECT 1

Mapping a Stream

To make an accurate map of a shallow stream, you'll need to set up a system of **transect** lines to help you survey the stream (see Figure 3). You'll need a hammer; twelve stakes; 120 meters (400 ft.) of lightweight cord or rope; a 30-meter (100-ft.) measuring tape; some flagging tape (or strips of fabric); a permanent marker; your journal; and a waterproof pen or pencil.

Select a 100-meter (330-ft.) stretch of a shallow stream that you can easily wade across. On the bank, hammer a stake into the ground at each end of the stretch. Tie the cord from stake to stake to establish a baseline. Along this baseline, use the flagging to mark six or more stations at equally spaced intervals. Number them consecutively with the marker.

Run a line, or transect, from each station across the stream. Each transect should be **perpendicular** to the baseline. To estimate a perpendicular line, stand at a station and

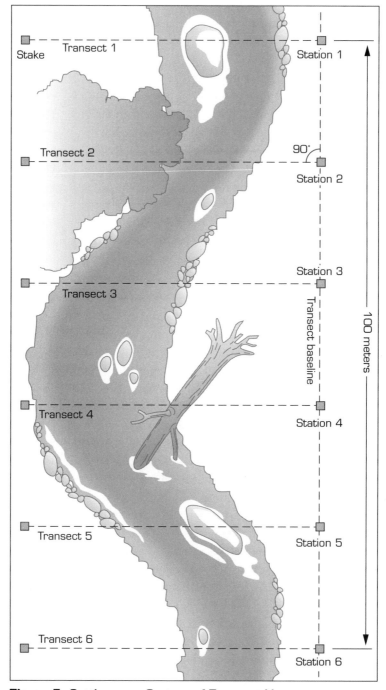

Figure 3 Setting up a System of Transect Lines

Table 1 Transect Line Data for Stream Mapping

Transect	Feature	Distance From Station
1	water's edge	5 m
1	boulder	7–7.5 m
1	tree cover	8–10 m

face the water. Hold your arms straight out to the sides, palms facing forward. Your arms should be parallel to the baseline. Sight along your right arm, making sure you are aligned with the baseline. Do the same on your left side. Now close your eyes and, with your fingers outstretched, bring your arms together in front of you until your palms touch. Open your eyes and sight along your arms and fingers. That line is perpendicular to the baseline.

Using this procedure, begin at Station 1 and sight a perpendicular line to a landmark on the opposite bank. Place a stake in the ground at that landmark and stretch a cord from Station 1 to that stake. Using the measuring tape, determine the distance from the station to the features you are including on your map, such as the water's edge or a fallen tree, and record the distances in your journal (see Table 1). Continue mapping by running transects across the creek from all the stations and taking measurements at each station.

When you have completed the measurements, you are ready to draw your map. It's easiest to work at home on a table or desk. You'll need paper, a protractor, a ruler, and a pencil.

First, choose a map scale. Maps are representations of real-life settings drawn on a smaller scale so that all the information fits on one page. Try letting 1 centimeter on the map equal 5 meters (1 in. = 30 ft.) in real measurement.

Now draw the baseline to scale. Mark and label the stations. Draw the transects, using a protractor to ensure they are perpendicular to the baseline. Using the information collected at each transect, mark the distances to key landmarks you wish to include on your map. Once all the distances are drawn to scale on your map, connect the points that represent the same feature. For example, connect all the points that represent the water's edge to show that feature on your map.

How Fast Does It Go?

A mountain river plunges down a rocky gorge, its water white with froth and spray. Miles away, a tea-colored stream laps at the bank as it snakes lazily through a swamp. Fast or slow, the waters of rivers and streams are constantly on the move. How fast do they move? Scientists measure their speed or velocity with an instrument called a flowmeter. You can make fairly accurate measurements, however, with a stopwatch; several stakes; a hammer (or several bricks with fishing bobbers attached using monofilament fishing line); and a 20-meter (66-ft.) measuring tape. You'll also need two friends and an object that floats (such as a lemon or an orange).

Pick a shallow stream that you can safely wade across. *Beware of slippery rocks and strong current! Play it safe—choose a stream with slow to moderate current.* Find a straight 20-meter (66-ft.) stretch of the stream that is clear of large boulders or fallen trees. Divide the section into three equal, parallel stretches—a central section and two side sections (see Figure 4 on the next page). Using a stake anchored

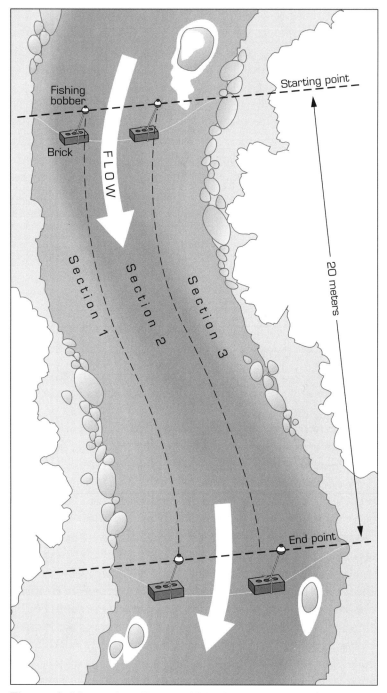

Figure 4 Measuring Current Velocity

Table 2 Measuring Current Velocity				
Segment	Trial	Distance	Time of Run	Stream Condition
1	1	20 m	22 seconds	riffle
1	2	20 m	18 seconds	riffle
1	3	20 m	24 seconds	riffle
1	4	20 m	21 seconds	riffle

in the streambed or a brick with attached fishing bobber, mark the starting and finishing point of each section.

To estimate current velocity, drop a float into the water in the middle of each section, upstream from the starting point. Time the float's run from start to finish. Repeat the trial at least four times, and discard any run in which the float moved out of the middle of the stream section being tested. Calculate an average time for the run by adding the times and dividing by the number of trials. Record the run times in your journal as shown in Table 2.

For each section, divide the total distance the float traveled by the average time it took. Calculate an average surface current velocity for the stream by adding the velocities of all three sections and dividing by three.

Estimate the stream's mean velocity (which represents an average for the stream at all depths and surface areas) by multiplying the average surface velocity by a correction factor: 0.8 for rough-bottomed streams with small or large stones; 0.9 for smooth-bottomed streams of sand, silt, mud, or solid bedrock.

$$\frac{\text{Distance float traveled per run}}{\text{Average time}} = \text{Current velocity}$$

$$\frac{\text{Average}}{\text{current velocity}} \times \frac{\text{Correction}}{\text{factor}} = \frac{\text{Mean current}}{\text{velocity}}$$

Which stream segment had the fastest current? A stream with a current velocity of 50 centimeters/second (20 in./sec) or greater is considered a fast-flowing stream. Is the stream you tested fast-flowing or slow-flowing?

✔ Doing More

Current velocity also varies with stream depth. Try taking velocity measurements using objects that sink lower in the water or stay on the water's surface. Can you determine the depth of the fastest-flowing water?

PROJECT **2**

Making a River Run*

Over thousands to millions of years, the flowing water of rivers and streams cuts slowly into Earth's crust to create valleys and canyons. To watch a high-speed version of this process, try making a model of your own river (see Figure 5). You'll need a plastic container (at least 8 × 2 × 6 centimeters [20 × 5 ×15 in.]); some **diatomaceous earth** (3.5 liters [14 cups]); a dust mask; water; a wood block (about 2.5 × 5 × 10 centimeters [1 × 2 × 4 in.]); a sponge; a plastic cup; scissors; a plastic coffee stirrer; 15 centimeters (6 in.) of 20-gauge (1-mm) wire; blue food dye; a measuring cup; dishwashing liquid; a stopwatch; your journal; and a pencil.

Diatomaceous earth is a material used in swimming-pool filters, but it also has other uses so be sure to use the kind made for pools. Look for it where swimming-pool supplies are sold.

---

*Modified from Kaufmann, Jeffrey, Robert C. Knott, and Lincoln Bergman. *River Cutters*, University of California at Berkeley, 1992.

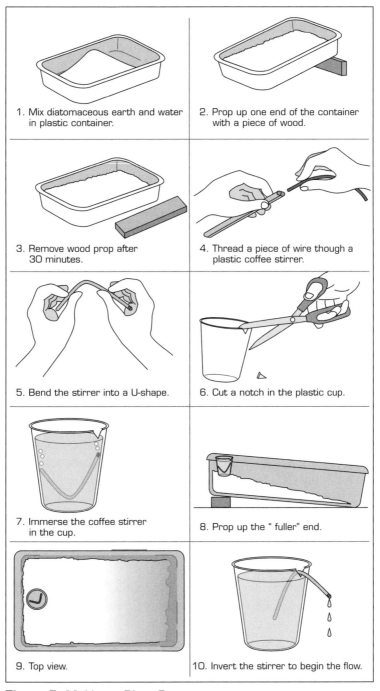

Figure 5 Making a River Run

With the dust mask covering your mouth and nose, measure 3.5 liters (14 cups) of diatomaceous earth into the plastic container. ***Be careful! The dust can be harmful to your lungs.*** Add 3 liters (12 cups) of water, and mix thoroughly with your hands. Rap the plastic container sharply on the table. Tilt one end up slightly (2 to 5 centimeters [1 to 2 in.]), shake the mixture to smooth the surface, and prop the tilted end up with a piece of wood. Let the mixture settle for 30 minutes, then remove the wood prop. Using a sponge, remove any excess water that has flowed to the bottom of the container.

Now prepare the dripper cup, which will act as the water source for your river. Cut a small notch into the rim of the plastic cup. To create the dripper, thread the piece of wire through the coffee stirrer so that the wire protrudes slightly on each end. Bend the stirrer into a U-shape. To make the liquid for the dripper cup, combine 0.5 liter (2 cups) of water; three to four drops of blue food dye; and two drops of dishwashing liquid. Fill the cup with the dyed water and immerse the U-shaped coffee stirrer until the bottom of the U touches the bottom of the cup. A few air bubbles will rise to the surface. Set the cup aside while you finish preparing the diatomaceous earth.

Now you are ready to let a river run. Prop up the higher end of the diatomaceous slope about 5 to 7 centimeters (2 to 3 in.). Push the dripper cup into the diatomaceous earth until it is level. To start the dripper system, quickly raise one end of the stirrer out of the water, leaving the other end immersed. Invert the stirrer and balance it in the notch of the plastic cup. Blue water should begin dripping out of the stirrer. Adjust the flow rate to about two drops per second by changing the curve of the stirrer.

Let the water run for 5 to 10 minutes. Watch carefully as the moving water erodes a channel through the earth. Try making quick sketches—or take a photograph—of the river every two minutes. How does the river change? Try to identify the geological processes of erosion, transport, and deposition.

The proportions of water and diatomaceous earth described here are just a starting point. If you live in a very dry area or a very humid area, add more or less water.

Don't get discouraged if the dripper system doesn't work on the first try. The problem may be a trapped air bubble. Reinvert the stirrer and tap it gently on the bottom of the cup to shake loose any bubbles.

Sorting it Out

Why are some steep mountain brooks strewn with large boulders and stones? Why are rivers in lower elevations usually sand- or silt-bottom channels? By constructing your own model stream, you can begin to answer these questions. You'll need polyvinyl chloride (PVC) piping (8 centimeters [3 in.] wide, and 300 centimeters [10 ft.] long); a jigsaw; spray adhesive; a chair or stepladder; a brick; masking tape; a garden hose with access to an outside faucet; a plastic container; a small measuring cup; and some samples of rock and earth in a range of sizes. Look for gravel or pebbles in the following size ranges: 3 to 5 centimeters (1 to 2 in.); 1 to 2 centimeters ($\frac{3}{8}$ to $\frac{3}{4}$ in.); and 0.5 centimeter ($\frac{1}{16}$ in.). Collect samples of sand and diatomaceous earth as well (see Project 2).

Cut the PVC piping in half lengthwise using the jigsaw. *Jigsaws are dangerous tools: be sure an adult helps you with this step.* Wipe the inner surface clean. Apply the spray adhesive to that area, a short section at a time. Dust the sticky areas with a layer of coarse sand, working your way down the entire length of the piping. Let the pipe section dry for at least one hour.

You have now constructed an artificial stream channel. To model a stream system from its mountainous passages to the lowlands, prop one end of the piping on the seat of a chair or the lower rung of a chair or stepladder. It should be about 50 centimeters (20 in.) off the ground. Place the lower end on a smooth surface such as a driveway or sidewalk. About 60 centimeters (24 in.) above the lower end of the piping, place a brick across the edges of the artificial channel to weigh it down and flatten it. At the upper end, tape the garden hose into position so that the water will run through the channel.

Combine a scoopful (about 0.1 liter [$\frac{1}{3}$ cup]) of rock, sand, or diatomaceous earth in an empty plastic container. Add water, shake, and then pour the materials into the upper end of the artificial channel.

Before you start the water flow from the garden hose, try to predict what will happen to the different-sized particles. Where will each end up? Jot down your predictions in your journal and include a sketch of your setup. Now slowly turn on the faucet so water trickles out of the hose. Watch what happens to the different rock particles. You can simulate a flood by increasing the flow a little more. Which rocks moved this time? How far did they move?

Panning for Gold

Playing around in streams is fun, but did you ever think it could make you rich? The California gold rush of 1849 began with the discovery of several flakes of gold in the gravel of a riverbed. Thousands of people flocked to the rivers and streams of the California mountains to seek their fortune.

A standard tool for those prospectors was a gold pan or miner's pan. With this simple piece of equipment, a small bottle, a magnifying lens, and some forceps, you too can prospect for gold. In mining areas, look for gold pans at a local hardware store. Or you can order pans from suppliers (see Appendix). You can also use a cooking pan or a large, broad plastic salad bowl with low-sloping sides.

Now that you have the equipment, where should you go to use it? Nevada, California, South Dakota, Utah, and Montana are the top gold-producing states in the United States. If you're already in a mining area, ask for advice at the local hardware store or United States Geological Survey (USGS) office. Use a **topographic map** to find a stream.

Once you're at a stream, look for sites in the channel bed just downstream from boulders or fallen trees, or along the inner bend of a curve. These are areas where heavy, dense materials—such as gold—carried by the fast-moving water, are dropped when the flow is slowed. Cracks and crevices in a solid-bedrock streambed are also good places to look for deposited materials.

Pan the material from these sites in the following way: Fill your pan half-full with sand, mud, and gravel from the stream bed. Submerge the pan in a slow section of the stream, then raise it above the water surface. Rap the pan sharply against a rock or other object to work the heavier objects to the bottom. Swirl the contents of the pan; let some water and finer **sediment** slosh out over the forward lip of the pan, away from you. Continue submerging the pan and swirling the contents until very little water or sediment remains. When you have only a spoonful of sediment left in your pan, use your magnifying lens and forceps to look for gold.

What will you see? Look for yellow or gold flakes about the size of the head of a straight pin. Do they shine in the sun? Shade that area of the pan with your hand. If the pieces still look shiny, try some other simple tests: Can you reshape the flakes with a hammer? If you scratch one with the tip of a knife, does the scratch look yellow? If the answer to these questions is yes, you may have found gold!

CHAPTER 2

From Drops to Trickles to Flash Floods: The Story of a Watershed

ON A HOT SUMMER DAY IN 1947, A young woman visiting the Great Smoky Mountains National Park spread her towel on a boulder at the bank of the Middle Prong of the Little River. She relaxed in the warmth of the sun, listening to the soothing sound of rushing water. Suddenly, the sound turned to a roar as a wall of turbulent water raced down the channel and swept the woman into the river.

Where did all that water come from? As the young woman was enjoying the peaceful setting, storm clouds were gathering over Thunderhead Mountain, several miles upstream. The dark storm clouds released a heavy rain that pelted the mountain forest. Then just as quickly, the clouds dispersed.

The rain that fell dripped off the leaves, flowed off the rocky slopes, and moved through shallow soils that were already soaked from previous rains. The water rapidly reached the mountain brooks nestled in the narrow valleys and rushed down the mountain. Meanwhile, in the lower valley, the sun was still shining on the banks of the river. By the time the rainwater reached the river, it was a mighty wall of churning, frothing liquid.

The land over which the rainwater traveled to reach the mountain brooks is called a **watershed.** Watersheds can be small or large, hilly or mountainous, or almost flat. Serving as **drainage basins** for rain or snowmelt, watersheds funnel water to a river, stream, lake, ocean, or wetland.

In the activities that follow, you'll learn how to map a watershed, determine its size, examine how soils affect watershed activities, and track how rapidly a watershed funnels rainwater through to its waterway. Understanding a watershed is basic to understanding a river or stream.

PROJECT **3**

Using Topographic Maps to Explore a Watershed

Because all the land on Earth is part of some watershed, everybody lives in one. Which watershed do you live in? To find out, try mapping the watershed of a nearby creek or stream. You'll need a highlighter, a pencil, a ruler, and a topographic map.

Most topographic maps of the United States are produced by the USGS. You can order their maps by calling (800) 435-7627. Map stores and camping-supply shops may also carry these maps. Ask for the 7.5-minute series, in which each map covers 7.5 minutes of longitude by 7.5 minutes of latitude.

Topographic maps look different from highway maps. They use symbols to represent buildings, quarries, cemeteries, and other features. Brown squiggly lines called **contour lines** help you visualize the shape of Earth's surface. These contour lines run all across the map to connect locations that are at the same elevation above sea level.

When contour lines are drawn close together, the slope of the land is steep. The elevation change between contour lines varies from map to map. On maps of flat country, the contour lines may represent 5-foot changes in elevation. On maps of mountainous areas, contour lines may show 100-foot changes. The change in elevation between contour lines is called the **contour interval.**

The heavier brown contour lines are called **index contour lines.** The number along the line indicates its elevation. Knowing the contour interval can help you determine the elevation of the lines between the index contours.

Understanding the contours of valleys and ridges is tricky. The contour lines of both of these geographic features form V-shaped patterns. To identify them, look for areas where several contour lines turn sharply, almost turning back on themselves. Trace an imaginary line down the middle of the V toward the point. If your line crosses contour lines that increase in elevation, that geographic feature is a valley or canyon. Streams or rivers may be found in these areas. Compare this to the contours of a ridge, where your imaginary line will cross lines that decrease in elevation (see Figure 6).

To see how well you understand topographic maps, pick two points on your map that are 5 to 7 centimeters (2 to 3 in.) apart. Mark each point with an X and connect them with a straight line. Imagine yourself hiking along the line you have drawn. At what elevation did you start? How many times did you go uphill or downhill? Did you go straight up or down a slope, or at an angle to the slope? What was your final elevation?

Are you ready to map a watershed? Spread your map out on a table and grab a highlighter, a pencil, and a ruler. You may want to photocopy and enlarge a portion of the map for this exercise. Find a first-order stream (a stream with no trib-

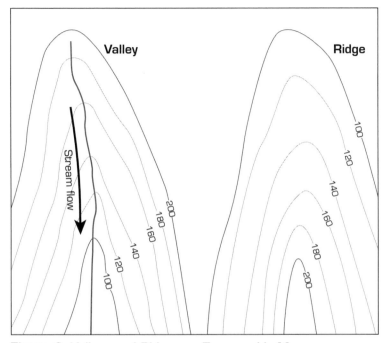

Figure 6 Valleys and Ridges on Topographic Maps

utaries) and highlight it. Using a pencil and a ruler, draw a series of lines perpendicular to the stream, spaced about 5 to 10 millimeters ($\frac{1}{4}$ to $\frac{1}{2}$ in.) apart. Also draw several lines radiating outward from the headwaters.

To mark the boundaries of the watershed, follow the lines you have drawn from the stream outward. Read the elevations as you cross index contours to determine whether you are traveling uphill. Continue following the line until it reaches a high point and then begins to decrease in elevation. At the highest elevation, place an X on the line. Repeat this procedure for every line you have drawn, all the way around the stream. Connect the X's to outline the boundary of your watershed (see Figure 7 on the next page).

Check your work by imagining a huge cloud raining over the area you have just circled. Where does the water go? Pencil in arrows on the map to indicate the direction of water flow. Keep in mind that water flows downhill, usually at right angles to contour lines. Look for areas with V-shaped con-

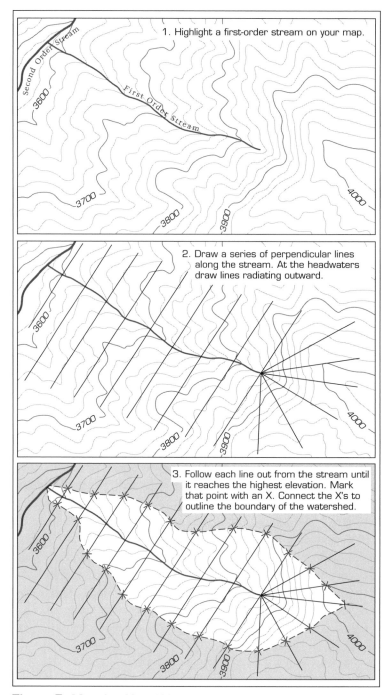

1. Highlight a first-order stream on your map.

2. Draw a series of perpendicular lines along the stream. At the headwaters draw lines radiating outward.

3. Follow each line out from the stream until it reaches the highest elevation. Mark that point with an X. Connect the X's to outline the boundary of the watershed.

Figure 7 Mapping Your Watershed

tours where the bottom of the V points to a higher elevation. Water will flow toward these areas.

How Big Is Your Watershed?

Watersheds come in all shapes and sizes. They can range in size from a few **hectares** to hundreds of millions of hectares (one hectare is about the size of two football fields).

You can measure your watershed using a clear sheet of acetate overlay or transparency film that you have marked with a grid. You'll need a fine-point permanent marker; a washable marker; a ruler; and a topographic map (7.5-minute series) with the boundaries of your watershed marked (see Project 3).

Begin by drawing a straight line along each edge of the transparency with the permanent marker. Find the kilometer bar scale on your map. Line up the upper-left corner of the transparency with the bar scale. Use the divisions on the scale to mark 0.1-kilometer (0.06-mile) units on the lines you have just drawn. When you have marked off ten of these divisions, slide the transparency film to the left and continue marking until you have finished the entire edge. Now rotate the film and use the scale to mark the remaining three edges of the transparency.

When all the edges are marked, use the ruler to connect the first markings on the right edge to the markings on the left edge. Continue down the page, connecting the pairs of points, to create a series of parallel lines across the page. Then draw a set of lines perpendicular to the first series by connecting the points at the top and bottom of the sheet. When laid over a 7.5-minute series topographic map, each small square of the grid outlines one hectare of land.

To use the grid, place it over the topographic map of your watershed. Count the number of whole squares that fall within the borders of the marked watershed. You may find it easier to count by using a washable marker to color the area of the watershed within the grid. Add up the number of colored squares. Don't forget to include the fractions of partially colored squares. The total is the area of your watershed, in hectares.

✔ Doing More

Get to know your watershed better. Walk or ride through the watershed to list the ways the land is being used. Map land-use activities (farming, residential, forested, commercial, or manufacturing) on your watershed map (see Figure 8). Using the transparency grid, estimate the percentage of the area devoted to each land-use activity. How might these activities affect the water quality or the quantity of water in a stream?

Become a watershed watchdog. Get involved with a local group of volunteers that monitors watershed activities. Con-

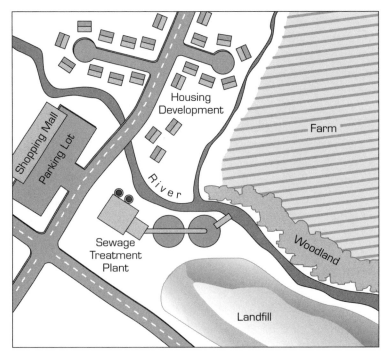

Figure 8 Land Use in Your Watershed

tact a local county or state environmental agency, the Natural Resource Conservation Service (under U.S. Government listings in the Blue Pages of your phone book), the Izaak Walton League of America, or the Adopt-A-Stream Foundation to find out about monitoring groups in your area (see the Internet Resources section at the back of this book).

How Much Water?

Turn on the faucet in your kitchen and watch as 3 to 5 gallons per minute swirl down the drain. At large springs as much as 5,000 gallons per minute or more may gush from an underground cavern. Sit on the bank of a creek or stream near your home and watch the running water. How much water flows there?

To estimate the flow of a shallow stream, grab your footgear; a measuring tape at least 20 meters (66 ft.) long; four stakes; a 2-meter (6.5-ft.) rod marked in centimeter intervals; a stopwatch; some oranges or lemons to use as floats; your journal; a pencil; and a calculator. ***Bring some friends, and ask an adult to accompany you, especially if you're going near fast-moving water. Review the water safety rules (see Introduction) before you go.***

At the creek, choose a straight 20-meter (66-ft.) stretch free of obstacles that might impede water flow. Mark the beginning and end of the stretch with stakes. Measure the width of the stream at the downstream end of the section by stretching a measuring tape across the stream. Record the stream width in your journal. Secure the tape to your stakes on the bank, and adjust it to make it level with the water surface and perpendicular to the direction of water flow.

Starting 0.5 meter (20 in.) from the water's edge, take depth measurements every meter (39 in.) using the 2-meter (6.5-ft.) measuring rod. Record this information in your journal. Move upstream to the midpoint and then to the end of the stream section. Take width and depth measurements at both places.

While your feet are still wet, grab your stopwatch and the floats. Follow the instructions in Investigation 2 to estimate current velocity. You now have all the data you need to estimate stream flow. Head to the creek bank, find your calculator, and let's start punching some numbers!

Use the width and depth measurements to calculate an average cross-sectional area of your stretch of the creek. Beginning with the downstream data, average the depth by adding the depth measurements together and dividing by the total number taken. Multiply the average depth by the width to estimate the cross-sectional area in square meters. Do the same for the remaining two sets of data from the middle and upstream end of the stretch. To calculate an average cross-sectional area for the entire stretch, add the three areas and divide by three.

Calculate an average adjusted current velocity using the information in Investigation 2.

Hang on, you're almost finished! Multiply the average cross-sectional area by the average adjusted velocity to obtain stream flow in meters^3/second. To visualize a flow rate of 1 meter^3/second, imagine a block of water 1 meter high, 1 meter wide, and 1 meter deep passing by you every second.

Rain, Snow, and Stream Flow: How Fast Does Your Watershed Drain?

A watershed funnels rain and snowmelt to its waterways. To find out how rapidly rain on your watershed ends up in the creek or stream near your home, you'll need a rain gauge; a measuring tape; a wooden dowel or metal rod (a metal fence post works well) measuring 120 to 180 centimeters (4 to

6 ft.); your footgear; a hammer; a waterproof marker; a pencil; your journal; and some graph paper. Select a shallow stream that you can access daily and whose watershed you've outlined (see Project 3).

Place a rain gauge in an open area within the watershed. You may wish to place several throughout the watershed. Inexpensive rain gauges can be purchased at discount chains or at lawn and garden-supply stores.

With a waterproof marker, mark the dowel or rod at 5-centimeter (2-in.) intervals. Number the 5-centimeter (2-in.) marks with consecutive numbers. Make the numbers large enough to be read from a distance.

To place a stream gauge in the stream, grab your footgear, the marked dowel or rod, and a hammer. ***Bring an adult along to assist you, especially if you're heading for a creek with fast-moving water. Think safety first! Review the water safety rules (see Introduction).*** Select a riffle area that is approximately 30 to 60 centimeters (12 to 24 in.) deep. Hammer the rod into the streambed. Be sure you can read the numbers on the stream gauge from the bank.

Begin monitoring stream and rain gauges during a short, dry spell at least 3 to 5 days after a rainstorm. Check the rain gauges and stream levels daily and record the information in your journal.

Now that you have some baseline data, keep an eye on the weather. Listen to the weather report to learn about approaching storms. From the onset of the first rainstorm, read the stream gauge and monitor the rain gauges every six hours (skipping nighttime hours). Empty the rain gauges after recording the volume of collected water. ***Read the stream gauge from the bank, staying clear of the rushing water. Watch your footing—the bank may be quite slippery or undercut by fast-moving water.*** Repeat these measurements for at least three days following the rain. How quickly does the stream reach its peak water level?

Scientists often present data on stream-flow changes in the form of a graph called a **hydrograph.** You can create your own hydrograph. Using plain graph paper, make two

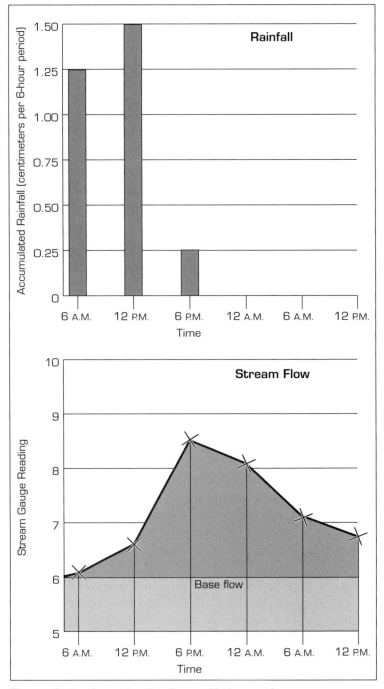

Figure 9 An Example of a Storm Hydrograph

stacked graphs. Plot the rainfall data on the *y-axis* of the top graph and the stream-gauge data on the *y-axis* of the bottom graph. Time (in hours) is on the *x-axis* of both graphs (see Figure 9).

Testing the Soil

Rain falling on a watershed is first received by plants and soils. The water's path is then largely determined by the type of soil over which it flows. Some soils readily absorb the excess water, while others are relatively impermeable, which results in surface runoff and flooding. What kinds of soils are found in your watershed?

You can test a soil's ability to hold water with some simple materials. You will need a shovel; several 1-gallon (3.8-liter) sealable plastic bags; a permanent marker; a large funnel; some cheesecloth; a stopwatch; a 2-liter clear plastic bottle (or 48-oz. juice bottle); a graduated cylinder or clear measuring cup; your journal; and a pencil.

To collect soil samples, choose a dry day several days after the last rainfall. Dig a small hole about 30 centimeters (12 in.) deep. Place some soil from the bottom of the hole in a sealable bag. Record the location of the hole in your journal and on the plastic bag.

Try to collect samples from many different places such as your backyard, a roadside, a riverbank, or a forest. If you go on vacation, take along a few plastic bags and collect soil samples there. Collect samples of sand, gravel, and clay as well. Lawn and garden stores or hardware stores offer a variety of materials. You can also use clay kitty litter as one of your samples.

To set up the experiment, plug the opening of the funnel with a small square of cheesecloth. Select one of your samples and add it to the funnel. Note the source of the sample

Table 3 Soil Drainage Data Sheet

Sample Type	Volume of Water Added	Time of First Drip	Time of Last Drip	Amount of Water Recovered
clay	200 mL	10 seconds	180 seconds	125 mL

in your journal. Support the funnel by setting it in the mouth of a large clear plastic bottle. To prevent a buildup of air pressure (which can affect your results), poke a few holes in the support bottle, near the mouth.

To test your soil sample, pour about 200 milliliters (1 cup) of water into the funnel and immediately start your stopwatch. Watch for puddling on the soil surface. Record the times of the first and last drip and the volume of water recovered in the plastic bottle. To simulate a second rain falling on wet soil, add an additional 50 milliliters ($\frac{1}{4}$ cup) of water and record the times of the first and last drips and the volume of water recovered. Repeat the experiment with each soil sample. Moisten the kitty litter and sand before testing them. Record your findings as shown in Table 3.

Which sample was the most **permeable?** Which absorbed the most water? From these results, can you predict which types of soil are more easily flooded?

✔ **Doing More**
Most soils are composed of sand, clay, and silt, as well as decaying plants and animals. Try these simple tests to classify your soil samples.

Table 4 Different Soil Types and Their Characteristics	
Type	Characteristics
silt	feels like powder when dry; slippery when wet; holds a mold wet or dry.
sand	holds together when wet but not when dry.
clay	holds together wet or dry; feels slippery or sticky

Wet a handful of soil and clench it tightly in your fist. Does it stick together well when wet? Does it stay together after it dries? Rub some soil between your thumb and forefinger. Does it feel gritty, sticky, or slippery (if wet) or like powder (if dry)? Rub a pinch of moistened soil against a coin while holding it up to your ear. Do you hear a sound? Is it faint?

As anyone who has ever spent a day at the beach with a pail and shovel knows, sandy soil holds a mold well when wet, but not when dry. This type of soil also feels gritty and makes a sound when rubbed against a coin. Clay soil holds together well when wet or dry and feels sticky or slippery when wet. Silty soil feels like powder or flour when dry and somewhat slippery when wet. Although it will hold a mold wet or dry, it can't be reshaped by rolling it between your hands. If you rub silty soil against a coin, you may hear a faint sound (see Table 4).

To learn more about the soils in your watershed, visit or call your local Natural Resources Conservation Service office (check your phone book for the U.S. Government listings, Department of Agriculture).

CHAPTER 3

From Top to Bottom and Side to Side: Who Lives There?

A GOOD WAY TO OBSERVE THE LIFE IN rivers and streams is to slip into a canoe and float downstream. As you drift over quiet pools you may catch a glimpse of small fishes lurking in the cool depths. Look at the water's edge and along quiet byways and backwaters for water striders and other surface creatures. Check for footprints along the bank, a record of visits by raccoons and otters. Reach over the side of your canoe and grab a small stone. The slippery, slimy coating on the rocks is made of microscopic organisms called **algae.** Look for large plants in the shallows. Their leaves and stems may sway in the wind, float on the water surface, or ripple and wave with the current.

Beneath It All

But you've still missed the most numerous group of stream dwellers. And they are right beneath you—hidden in the crevices of the rocky streambed, on the undersides of stones, and even in the sand and mud. A 30-centimeter^2 (1-foot^2) area may house more than 4,000 of these creatures!

Who are these hidden creatures? Most of these bottom dwellers are **invertebrates**—animals that don't have backbones. They range in size from 1 millimeter to several centimeters (up to 2 in.). Most are the **larvae** or immature stages of insects that live on land as adults. Hatched from eggs laid in the stream by adult females, these insects go through several stages of development before they transform into winged adults. They spend most of their life in the streambed. Many live for only a few hours or days as adults.

Many insect larvae make their homes in the riffles of gravel-bed streams. Turn over a large stone and examine its underside. You may catch a glimpse of a dark, flattened, cricket-like insect with two long feathery tails scuttling across the rock's surface. This is a stonefly larva.

Small tube-shaped collections of tiny pebbles, sand grains, or pieces of twigs or leaves may also be attached to the stone. These

A favorite meal for trout, stonefly nymphs are common in clean, cold, fast-flowing water.

The home of this caddisfly larva is a tube constructed of pieces of leaves. Some caddisfly larvae construct houses of small stones or pieces of sand.

are the dwellings of caddisfly larvae. Look closely and you may see a caterpillar-like creature poking its head and front legs out of the opening. Deeper in the streambed, down among the sand grains, you'll find mayfly larvae with paddle-like feet, tusks used for digging, and a hairy coat that helps them breathe.

Even the muddy river bottom has its share of invertebrate critters. Slender wormlike midge larvae, some only a few millimeters long, live in the sand and mud, feeding on debris that settles to the river bottom. Often as many as 50,000 occupy a single square meter (1 sq. yd.). Nearby, a bed of mussels filters the river water, feeding on microscopic plants and animals. Relatives of the earthworm can be found here also, building vertical tubes that protrude from the river bottom.

PROJECT 5

Making an Insect Rearing Cage

To study the life cycle of an aquatic insect, you could set up an aquarium at home. But mimicking the conditions of a swiftly flowing stream is difficult. Instead, why not set up an insect cage in the stream itself? To construct the cage you'll need some aluminum window screening; a ruler; wire clippers or an old pair of scissors; some tags; and a waterproof marker (see Figure 10 on the next page).

Cut a 46-centimeter (18-in.) square from a piece of window screening using a finished edge as one side of the square. Bring the two parallel cut edges of screening together to form a cylinder. Make a seam along the length of the cylinder by folding the edges 1.5 centimeters ($\frac{1}{2}$ in.), and then folding them again, as if you were closing a paper lunch bag. With the finished edge of screening at the top, close the bottom by making two 1.5-centimeter ($\frac{1}{2}$-in.) folds.

Turn over a large stone in a rocky streambed to find an aquatic insect. Many of these creatures move fast, so be quick. Carefully place one insect and a small stone or two in the wire cage. Close the opening by folding the edges as before. Attach a tag to the cage, and number it with a waterproof marker. Set the cage upright in the stream so that half of the cage is above the water surface.

Make biweekly or monthly visits to the cage to track the insect's life cycle. Record the insect's length during each visit. Look for the hard, outer shells, called **exoskeletons,** that have been shed during a **molt.** Most aquatic insects molt several times during the larval period. You may see a dormant or dead-looking larva wrapped in a cocoonlike case. This is the **pupa,** or pupal stage. While it is not characteristic of all life cycles, it does signal the end of **metamorphosis** for some animals. Figure 11 on page 47 shows the life cycle of a common stream inhabitant—a midge.

How long will you have to wait to see the adult? Life cycles vary from less than 2 weeks to 3 or 4 years. In coldwater streams in North America, a yearly cycle is common. Look for slow larval growth during the winter and maturation in early spring. Try to identify the adult using a field guide (see the section headed For Further Information at the back of this book for a list of suggested guides).

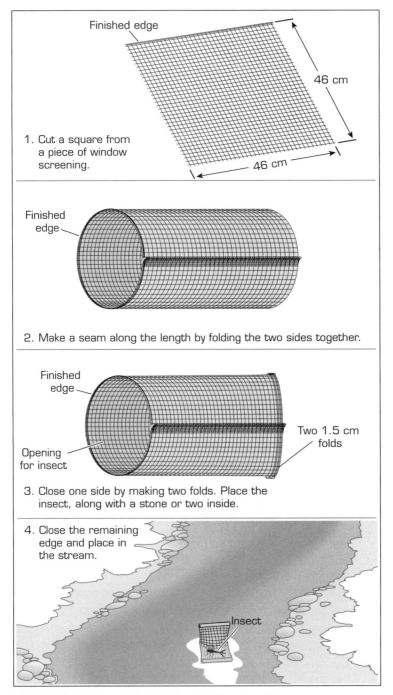

1. Cut a square from a piece of window screening.

46 cm

46 cm

Finished edge

Finished edge

2. Make a seam along the length by folding the two sides together.

Finished edge

Two 1.5 cm folds

Opening for insect

3. Close one side by making two folds. Place the insect, along with a stone or two inside.

4. Close the remaining edge and place in the stream.

Insect

Figure 10 Constructing an Insect Rearing Cage

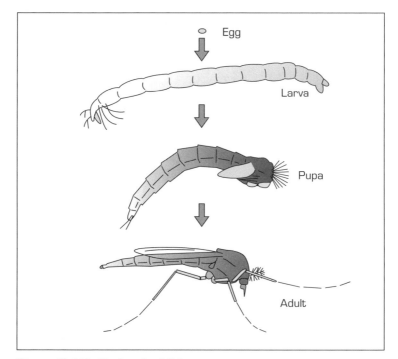

Figure 11 Life Cycle of a Midge

PROJECT **6**

Creatures in Hiding: Using a Kick Net

To quickly flush out an assortment of **benthic** stream dwellers, visit a shallow gravel-bed stream with a kick net. Pack up your footgear; a kick net (see Appendix for information about making your own); forceps; some white plastic trays; collecting jars; and a white sheet (optional). If you are interested in identifying what you find, see Figure 12 on pages 48–49 or the section headed For Further Information at the back of this book for suggested field guides. *Invite a few friends along, and before you go, be sure to review the water safety rules (see Introduction).*

Once you're at a stream, wade upstream with the kick net until you reach a riffle. Have a friend push the ends of the

Figure 12 A Sampling of Aquatic Invertebrates

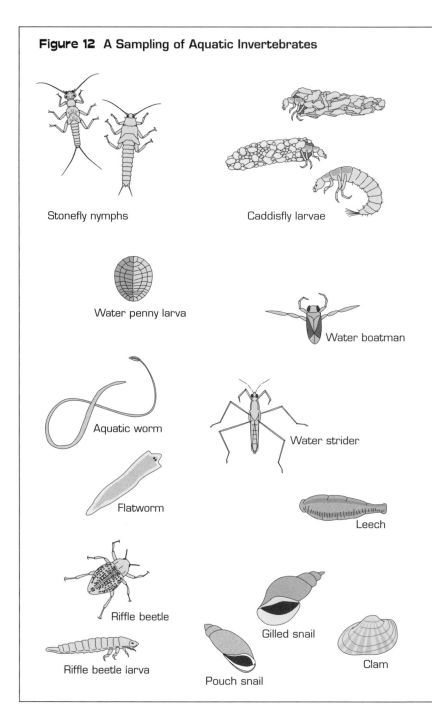

Stonefly nymphs

Caddisfly larvae

Water penny larva

Water boatman

Aquatic worm

Water strider

Flatworm

Leech

Riffle beetle

Gilled snail

Riffle beetle larva

Clam

Pouch snail

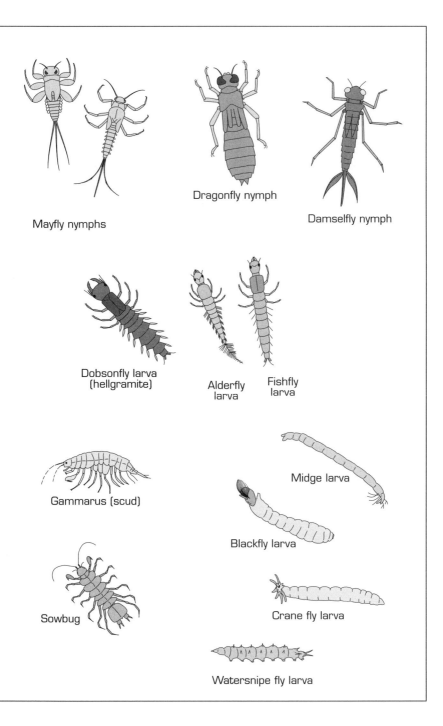

Mayfly nymphs

Dragonfly nymph

Damselfly nymph

Dobsonfly larva
(hellgramite)

Alderfly
larva

Fishfly
larva

Gammarus (scud)

Midge larva

Blackfly larva

Sowbug

Crane fly larva

Watersnipe fly larva

wooden slats of the kick net into the streambed so that the bottom edge of the net is nestled in the gravel. The net should be tilted slightly downstream. Standing just upstream from the net, pick up some stones and turn them over. Gently rub the surface of each stone to loosen any small creatures, and let the current wash them into the kick net. To capture the creatures burrowed into the streambed, dig your heels into the rocky bottom, and shuffle your feet back and forth for a minute or two.

Reach into the stream and grab the bottom edge of the kick net as your friend lifts it out of the water. Don't let water wash over the top end of the net or you may lose your catch. Carry the net back to the bank and lay it on the ground. To make it easier to see some of the really small critters, you may want to place the net on a white sheet. With forceps or tweezers, pick out anything that moves and put it into a shallow white tray containing stream water. What kinds of animals have you found? How many different kinds are there? Use a field guide to identify them. Collect a few specimens to take with you and return the others to the stream.

✔ Doing More

Stream invertebrates can also be sampled by placing artificial surfaces, or **substrates,** in the stream. After several weeks, the artificial substrate will be colonized by a variety of stream creatures. See the Appendix for directions on making a simple artificial substrate sampler—the Hester-Dendy sampler.

Sampling Sandy-Bottomed Streams

Not all creatures hidden in the streambed live in a riffle. Some can be found at the silty bottom of a pool or at the bottom of a slow-moving stream or river. Collecting these creatures requires a D-frame aquatic net (see Appendix for instructions for constructing one); some shallow white trays; forceps; a plastic squirt bottle; a hand lens; and collecting jars. Identify the creatures you catch with a field guide to aquatic invertebrates.

Try sampling for insects in protected areas just down-stream from a bridge piling, boulder, tree trunk, or over-hanging bank. Push the flat edge of the aquatic net 7 to 10 centimeters (3 to 4 in.) into the soft sediment and scoop up a small sample. Sieve out the silt and sand by partially sub-merging the net in the stream and swishing it back and forth. Pick out any rocks or plant debris by hand. Once the sample is free of sediment and debris, dump it into a shallow white tray. Remove any creatures still clinging to the net by wash-ing them into the tray with the squirt bottle. Spread the col-lected material into a thin layer. Using a hand lens if necessary, pick out any wriggling stream creatures with for-ceps and place them in collecting jars containing stream water. Use the squirt bottle to keep the sample wet as you are sorting. What kinds of creatures have you collected? (See Figure 12. For suggested field guides, check the section headed For Further Information at the back of this book.)

✔ Doing More

To separate stream invertebrates from sand, silt, and rock, try suspending them in a dense sugar solution. Add a 5-pound bag of sugar to 2 gallons of water and mix well. Stir your sample into the sugar solution. Because their bodies are less dense than the sugar solution, stream animals will float while the sediment sinks. Using a fine-mesh aquarium net, scoop the floaters from the top. Rinse the netted animals into a shallow white tray to study them.

Life in the Fast Lane

Hidden among pieces of leaf debris a caddisfly spins its silken net. Upstream a mayfly braces against the surface of a stone, holding its front legs directly into the current. The long bristles of its legs intermesh, forming a makeshift basket.

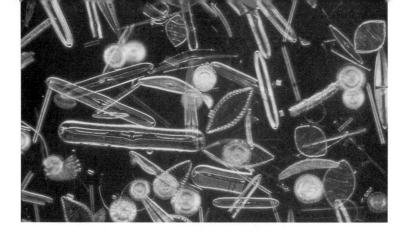

Diatoms are single-celled organisms that construct protective shells of an elaborate design.

What are these stream creatures trying to catch in their nets or baskets? Food! The current carries a rich source of animal and plant material in the form of **drift.** Drift consists of living and dead animals and plants, and smaller organisms that float or swim weakly in the current.

Floating or swimming, plant or animal, microscopic or macroscopic, these small stream dwellers are called **plankton.** Some of the most common plankton creatures are **diatoms**—one-celled organisms with intricate shells made of silica. Diatoms come in an amazing variety of geometric shapes, and each shell is finely etched with radiating lines, spines, or ridges.

Scuds are common shrimplike animals that graze on diatoms during the day. They are another component of plankton. At night, scuds scavenge on both large and small food particles (see Figure 12).

PROJECT **8**

Netting Invisible Stream Life:
How to Use a Plankton Net

Dip a jar into the backwater of a river or stream and you might be lucky enough to capture a few microscopic creatures. But pull a plankton net through the water and you're sure to net a whole host of unusual and fascinating, minute organisms.

To study these tiny creatures, you'll need a plankton net (you can buy one or make one yourself, see Appendix); appropriate footgear; a stopwatch; a squirt bottle; some collecting jars; an ice chest; a **compound microscope;** a pipette or medicine dropper; and some microscope slides and cover slips.

The best place to find plankton is in a slow-moving stream or river. Channels that drain bodies of standing water such as marshes, swamps, and lakes are also rich in plankton. *If you choose to sample river plankton, work from a dock, pier, or the bank. Use common sense around deep water, and review the water safety rules before you begin (see Introduction).*

Begin sampling by placing your net in the water with the opening facing into the current. In very slow current flows, tow the net by hand or from a canoe or rowboat. The size of the plankton population and the speed of the current will determine the length of time you need to leave the net in the water. Typical hauls range from 1 to 10 minutes. Use a stopwatch to time each sample.

To retrieve the sample, pull the net vertically out of the water without letting the water slosh over the rim. Let the water drain down through the net until about 50 milliliters ($\frac{1}{4}$ cup) of water remains. Rinse down the inner walls with the squirt bottle to catch any creatures clinging there. If you made your own net, untie the string and let the sampler contents flow into a small container. For purchased nets, detach the sample bottle. The brownish-green material you see is the plankton. For best results, keep your sample cool with ice and examine the plankton within four hours.

To view these tiny organisms, you'll need to borrow a compound microscope from your school science lab. Ask your science teacher to help you use the microscope. Swirl the plankton sample gently for several minutes. With a pipette or medicine dropper, retrieve a sample from mid-depth, avoiding any large clumps or particulate matter. Place a drop of the sample in the center of a clean microscope slide and cover it with a coverslip. You are now ready to explore the fascinating world of planktonic creatures.

✔ **Doing More**

Many of the creatures you'll see are diatoms. Their beautiful siliceous shells can best be seen by first removing the living cell structures inside, using heat. To do this, you'll need some microscope slides and coverslips; a test-tube holder or wooden clothespin; and a Bunsen burner.

Place a large drop of the diatom sample on a clean microscope slide. Using a test-tube holder or clothespin, hold the slide over a Bunsen burner flame for a few seconds while the water boils. Let the slide cool, then add a drop of tapwater and cover the preparation with a coverslip. Now look at the slide under a compound microscope.

Go Fish

Life in the fast lane isn't restricted to the plankton. Lurking in the cool depths are the most familiar inhabitants of running water—the fishes.

A darter hides in a crevice of a mountain brook's rocky bed as it watches what the current brings. With a burst of lightning speed, this minnowlike fish thrusts its body into the current, grabs a small insect, and retreats to another sanctuary. Farther down the mountain, where pools and riffles predominate, the trout is king. This large, streamlined fish is the primary predator in this part of the stream. As the stream water warms up during its downhill run, trout and other cold-water fishes give way to warm-water **species.** Schools of minnows frequent the open water, while sunfish lurk in weed beds, and a largemouth bass hovers under a fallen log. Where the stream becomes a river, the nocturnal catfish creeps along the muddy bottom, using its whiskers to locate food. See Figure 13 for drawings of some common stream fishes.

Many species of fishes live in rivers and streams. Half of all animals with backbones—the **vertebrates**—are

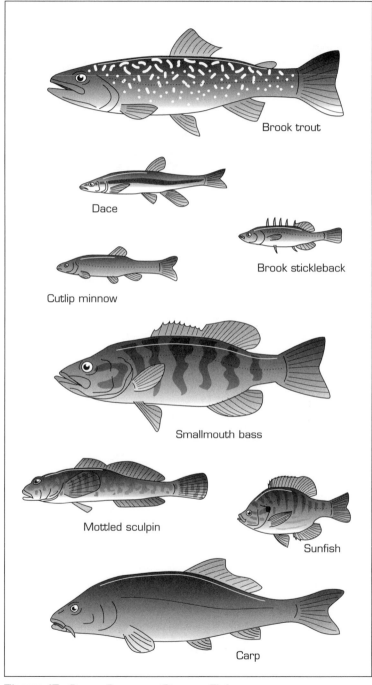

Figure 13 Some Common Stream Fishes

While usually considered a lake fish, largemouth bass also inhabit slow-moving streams and rivers. They often take cover in weed beds and under fallen trees.

fishes. Try the activities that follow to get to know these finned critters.

Shadows in the Water:
How to Observe the Fishes

With a little luck and perseverance, you can learn a lot about the fishes in a stream without using a rod and reel. You'll need binoculars; a field guide to freshwater fishes (see the section headed For Further Information at the back of this book); and a pair of polarized sunglasses to reduce the glare from the water's surface.

Rivers are generally so deep that fishes are hard to spot, so head to a nearby stream. It is easier to see the fishes if you are far above the water (bridges and high banks are good viewing sites). Choose a time when the sun is high and the sky is clear.

Are you in position? Now that you have a front-row seat, what can you see? Nothing? The trick is knowing where to look. Fishermen call this "reading the water." Most types of fishes prefer cool temperatures and slow currents. They like to be out of the main current but close enough to grab a passing morsel. Look for fishes in the still pockets just downstream of boulders, fallen trees, and bridge pilings. Deep pools and weedy areas are also good spots. You might also want to try looking along the outer bend of a channel where the stream has undercut the bank.

As you stare into the water, watch for shadows or a glint of silver against the light-colored streamed. Can you make out the general shape of the body? Look for parts of a fish, such as a head, a tail, or fins—sometimes you can't see the whole fish. To identify the fish, try to get a glimpse of its sides: most distinctive markings are located here. Wait patiently, sooner or later your fish will roll slightly to one side or the other.

✔ Doing More

Observing reproductive behavior in the spring and early summer is easy and rewarding. Most species of sunfish nest in shallow water. Look for depressions in the streambed that may appear cleaner than the surrounding area. Here the males court passing females. You may witness spawning or a group of young fish.

PROJECT **10**

Surveying Fishes

What types of fishes live in a creek or stream near your home? Surveying the fishes in a small stream can be done with a rod and reel, but a more efficient and reliable method involves using large flat nets called **seines**. In many states, you will need a special collecting permit or a valid fishing license to use a seine. Check with your local fish and wildlife commission to find out what your state requires.

A minnow seine can be purchased at a bait shop or a sporting goods store. Look for a 1.2 × 3 meter (4 × 10 foot)

Seining is hard work!

seine with 6 millimeter ($\frac{1}{4}$-in.) mesh. You will need a meter stick; a hammer; some stakes; some large clean buckets; suitable footgear; your journal; a pencil; and several friends. Find a shallow wadeable stream to study. ***Before you begin, be safety-conscious. Review the water safety rules (see Introduction).***

Start with a section of stream about the length of a pool or riffle area, approximately 20 meters (66 ft.). After marking the beginning and end with stakes, walk along the bank to the upstream end of the stretch with a friend and your seine. Grab one pole of the seine while your friend takes the other. Stretch the netting across the stream so that the seine completely blocks the passage of the fishes. The weighted bottom edge of the seine should be flush with the streambed.

Slowly walk downstream dragging the bottom edge of the seine along the streambed, angling the seine slightly in an upstream direction. At the downstream end of the stretch, carefully lift the seine out of the water horizontally to retain the trapped fishes, or have your partner slowly walk the seine toward the bank and land the fishes there. Seining takes lots of practice, so don't get discouraged if you're not successful on the first try.

Place the fishes you have netted in water-filled buckets to study them. Use your field guide to identify the species. Count the number of each species. Measure the lengths of the fishes from the tip of the snout to the base of the tail. Work quickly and keep your hands wet while handling the fishes. Touching a fish with dry hands may remove some of its protective slime and leave it susceptible to infection by bacteria and fungi. Return the fishes to the stream when you have completed and recorded your observations in your journal.

✔ **Doing More**
Surveys of fishes can also be done underwater using scuba gear or a mask and snorkel. Take a crayon and wear a short piece of PVC piping on your wrist to record your observations.

Walking on Water

Far above the fishes, where the water meets the air, water molecules cling tightly to one another. They form a thin film that's strong enough to support some very special creatures.

Water striders can be found on slow-moving water almost everywhere in the world, so chances are you live close to these water walkers. Look for long-legged insects with dark, thin bodies. Usually seen in groups on quiet, shady waters close to the bank, these insects glide across the water surface as they hunt for prey.

Even the fast-moving water of a stream riffle is home to at least one surface bug, the broad-shouldered water-bug or riffle bug, a cousin of the common water strider. Equipped with retractable claws, a velvety coat of tiny hairs, and a plumelike cluster of feathery hairs that can be spread out across the water surface, the riffle bug goes where few other insects can venture in its search for food and mates.

The smallest of the water walkers, the springtail,

prefers quieter waters. Springtails are often seen huddled together in patches about the size of your hand along stream banks. Each springtail is about the size of a flake of pepper. If you try to sweep them off the water surface with a net, you'll be surprised at how fast they move! Using a paddle-shaped structure held beneath the body, springtails propel themselves into the air, jumping as high as fifteen times their body length.

PROJECT **11**

Catching Insects on the Water's Surface

The water striders and their fellow water walkers may be tricky to catch, but they are worth the effort. Using an aquatic net (see Appendix to learn how to construct one), scoop them off the water surface with a rapid downstream sweep. Because these insects have good eyesight, they may see the net coming and move to avoid it. You may have more luck if you submerge the net in the water and jerk it straight up when an unsuspecting strider glides past.

If the wily springtail still eludes you, set up a pan trap. To make a simple pan trap, you'll need a shallow, white plastic pan or tray; a metal clip; a hammer; a stake; 60 to 90 centimeters (24 to 36 in.) of rope; and some dishwashing liquid. Attach the metal binding clip to one side of the white tray. Tie one end of the rope to the clip and the other end to a stake driven into the stream bank. Add some stream water and a squirt of detergent to the tray. Float the trap in an area where you've seen springtails congregate.

Detergents interfere with the bonds that form between water molecules at the surface and weaken the thin film that supports creatures like springtails and water striders. Any springtail that lands in the pan trap will drown. Use a hand lens and forceps or tweezers to examine these wingless acrobats.

Caring for a Live Water Strider

Have you ever watched a water strider stab helpless prey with its needle-like beak, or groom its body hairs with its built-in comb? Set up an aquarium for these insects and you'll be able to observe their behavior.

If you manage to catch a mating pair of water striders, you'll be able to raise a new generation in your own home. If you can't catch any yourself, you can order water striders from many biological supply houses from March through November (see the section headed For Further Information at the back of this book).

To rear these water bugs, you'll need an aquarium or a clear plastic container. The minimum size of the container depends on the size of the water striders you want to keep. A mating pair require a 5-gallon aquarium filled to a depth of 10 centimeters (4 in.) with distilled water. Small species and immature forms will do well in a smaller container. Plan on about 4 to 8 liters (1 to 2 gal.) of water per pair of insects.

Tiny, water-repellent hairs and long legs help keep these water striders walking on water.

Water striders are quite agile, so be sure to cover the containers with window screening. Keep the temperature between 21 and 24°C (70 and 75°F).

These water walkers are predators that patrol the water surface looking for prey. Their diet includes terrestrial insects that have fallen on the water and small invertebrates just below the surface. Feed your captive striders freshly killed insects every day. If you are raising large adult mating pairs, feed them a few crickets. You can buy crickets from a local bait shop. Smaller water striders will be quite happy with smaller prey such as fruit flies.

You can raise fruit flies by placing a small jar containing an overripe piece of banana or strawberry on a window ledge outside of your house. The flies will feed on the fruit in your jar and lay their eggs there. To collect a few flies to feed to the striders, take a matching empty jar with a lid and invert it over the culture jar. Tap the bottom jar to bring some flies into the top jar. Quickly remove the top jar and cap it. Place it in the freezer for 15 minutes. At feeding time, simply tap the fruit flies out of the jar onto the water surface. Adult striders may need three to four fruit flies a day, while immature striders will need only one.

If you want to keep the striders for a long period of time, set up an aquarium with a filter and pump. This will keep the water aerated and free of harmful bacteria. If you don't have a filter and pump, you'll have to change the water frequently. Use a small aquarium net to move the striders while you clean their aquarium. Be careful—these insects may try to stab you with their sharp beaks!

With a mating pair, you'll be able to observe the entire life cycle of these creatures. But they'll need a place to lay their eggs. Pieces of cork or Styrofoam provide suitable egg-laying surfaces. The female deposits between 20 and 40 eggs on the undersides of floating objects. The tiny eggs, only 1 to 2 millimeters ($\frac{1}{8}$ in.) long, hatch in a week. Because water striders are often cannibalistic, separate the newly hatched young from the adults.

At the Water's Edge

Water striders, riffle bugs, and springtails spend most of their lives on the water surface, relying on the water's invisible skin to support their body weight. Where do these creatures go when that surface is rippled by rain or when the water is frozen?

They go to the water's edge and hide under the leaf litter on the stream bank, or among the plants growing in the shallows. Rivers and streams support a wide range of plant life—from mosses to flowering plants. A variety of bacteria and **protists,** such as algae, are also found close to shore.

Many slow-moving streams or rivers, especially those in the southern United States, have extensive beds of flowering plants at their edges, and they often form distinct longitudinal zones along the shore line (see Figure 14 on the next page). Close to the bank, plants like the familiar cattail send tall, slender leaves up into the air, while their roots remain firmly planted in the streambed. Adjacent to this area is a zone of floating-leaved plants. With true leaves and roots that float on the water surface, plants like duckweed or water hyacinth get everything they need from the sun, the air, and the water.

In clear running waters, an inner zone of submersed plants is common. Here the straplike leaves of eel grass form huge underwater beds that ripple and wave with the current. Rooted in the streambed, these plants send their leaves upward. Some submergents, like pondweed, have two types of leaves: some that remain underwater and some that float on the water surface.

Hundreds of miles upstream, high in the mountains, the plant life changes. Dark green, feathery carpets of moss cover boulders and smaller stones. Long, bright-green filaments of green algae trail in the current. Everywhere in the shallows, the **periphyton**—a thin layer of microscopic algae and bacteria that grows on hard surfaces—coats the rocks of the streambed.

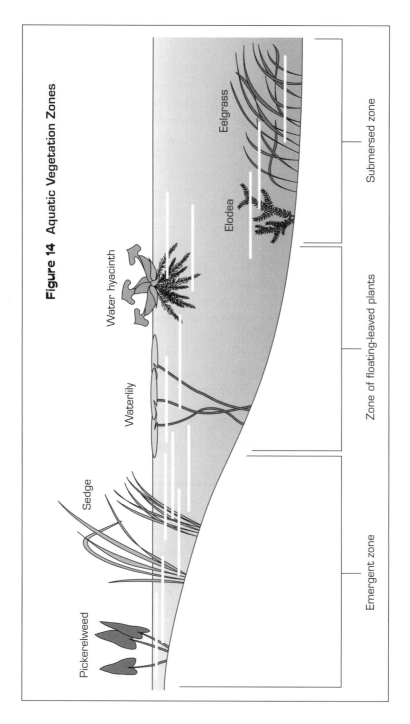

Figure 14 Aquatic Vegetation Zones

Pickerelweed

Sedge

Waterlily

Water hyacinth

Elodea

Eelgrass

Emergent zone

Zone of floating-leaved plants

Submersed zone

Use the activities that follow to explore the amazing world of aquatic plants, protists, and bacteria. What plants can you find in your neighborhood stream? Be a science detective—can you find any small creatures hidden among the plants? You might be surprised at what you see.

INVESTIGATION **8**

Sampling the Greens: Examining the Macrophytes of Rivers and Streams

To study the macroscopic plants, or **macrophytes,** of rivers and streams, you'll need a weed hook (see Appendix for directions on how to make your own); a ruler; some plastic bags; a measuring stick; your journal; a pencil; and a field guide to aquatic plants.

Using a topographic map or highway map, locate a nearby river or large stream. Look for easy access points, such as a boat landing or a bridge. Before you go, find out from local county or state officials if any aquatic plants in the region are protected. If so, you'll be prohibited from collecting samples of those plants.

As you approach a plant bed, note the variety and abundance of plants. Try estimating the area of each zone. Sketch leaf shapes and other features in your journal. Refer to the field guide to help you identify the plants. (See the section headed For Further Information at that back of this book for a list of suggested guides.)

To retrieve samples, tie the weed hook to a cast line. Attach the other end of the line to a fixed object and toss the weed hook into the middle of the plant bed. Let the weed hook sink, then slowly begin pulling it toward you.

If you are collecting plant material to examine later, wash off the mud and silt before placing the plants in a plastic bag. Close the bag tightly and label it with the sampling site, date, and time.

✔ Doing More

The plants growing in the shallows provide food and shelter for a wide variety of small creatures. Can you find any of them among the aquatic plants of a nearby stream or river? You will need an aerial insect net; an aquatic net or a kitchen strainer taped to a broom handle (use strong, water-resistant tape such as duct tape); some collecting jars; a field guide to aquatic life; and a hand lens. ***Be safe—ask an adult to accompany you.***

To minimize disturbance, approach the plant bed in a boat. Beat the aerial stems and leaves for insects with the insect net. Sweep the aquatic net through the water, brushing the underwater vegetation. You can best examine the undersides of floating or submerged leaves by hand. Use a field guide to aquatic life to identify your finds.

PROJECT **13**

The Green, Green Grass of a Stream Home: Making a Periphyton Sampler

A larval caddisfly, all but hidden inside its stone-studded case, grazes on a lush field that covers a streambed. Nearby, a snail does the same. What are they eating? Periphyton—the algae and bacteria that grow on hard surfaces in the stream.

To view the microscopic creatures that make up the periphyton, make your own sampler (see Figure 15). Collect several plastic baskets like the kind used in dishwashers (they should have a minimum width of 10 centimeters [4 in.]); several small metal binding clips from an office-supply store; some microscope slides; a waterproof marker; some flagging; a rope; wire cutters; and something to use as a weight (a brick works well). A basket that measures 20 × 10 centimeters wide (8 × 4 in.) will hold five microscope slides. You'll also need a single-edged razor blade and a microscope to view the periphyton.

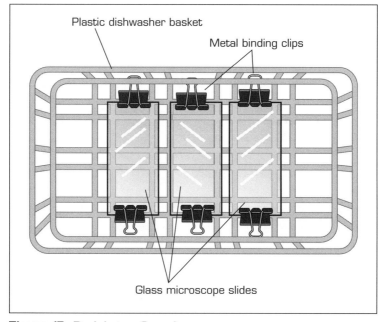

Figure 15 **Periphyton Sampler**

Number the edge of each microscope slide with a waterproof marker. Open the plastic basket and place the slides on the bottom, side by side. Secure each slide to the basket with one metal binding clip. If the clips won't fit between the bars of the basket, modify the basket with wire cutters.

To collect a good periphyton sample, locate a riffle in a gravel-bed stream. Examine the streambed for periphyton growth—look for a greenish-golden covering with a slippery, slimy feel. Now position the rack in the riffle at a depth of 30 to 60 centimeters (12 to 24 in.). Tie the rack to a brick or other weight to ensure that the sampler remains in place for several weeks. Mark its location by tying a piece of flagging to a nearby tree.

Check the sampler weekly to make sure it has not been dislodged. Carry a plastic peanut-butter jar and a cooler with you. Each week remove one microscope slide to examine at home or in your science lab at school. Keep the slide com-

pletely submersed in stream water and on ice as you transport it. In most streams you should see good periphyton
growth by about four weeks.

If your slides become coated with sediment after you
place them in the streambed, reposition the basket so that
the slides are positioned vertically rather than horizontally.
Only the narrow sides of the slides should face into the water
current.

To examine the slides, scrape one surface clean with a
razor blade, then place the slide on the stage of a compound
microscope, clean side down. If you're unfamiliar with this
type of microscope, ask your science teacher to assist you.
Use a field guide to freshwater algae to identify what you find
(see Appendix).

Vertebrate Visitors

Rivers and streams attract some special feathered and
furry creatures. They come, not as passersby to ad-
mire the cool, inviting water, but as predators, living on
the life within the water.

The startling cry of the belted kingfisher may be the
only sign that this feathery predator is nearby. Look for
these attractive blue-and-white birds on tree branches
high above woodland streams. Spying a small fish near
the surface, this bird dives headlong into the water to retrieve it.

Although the kingfisher's performance may be
splashier, that of the dipper, or water ouzel, is no less unusual. Found in the clear mountain streams of the western United States, bobbing up and down on its short
stubby legs as it peers into the rushing water, the dipper
seeks its prey on the streambed. With a short hop it
plunges into the current and scrambles along the
streambed as it searches among the small stones for insect larvae and other small creatures.

The belted kingfisher makes its home along rivers and streams in North America. Besides fishing the water, these birds raise their young in nests tunneled into rivers and stream banks.

Preying upon those same bottom dwellers is a small, furry creature seldom seen by humans. The water shrew, a small mammal with a mouse-like body and a long, narrow snout, usually remains hidden along the banks of streams or ponds. It enters the water only to hunt for food. Standing underwater, with its feet kicking, the shrew roots along the bottom, searching for insects. After a brief time, the animal rights itself and bobs to the surface.

Almost as elusive as the water shrew is the sleek river otter, found along rivers and streams in most parts of

Although they are mostly nocturnal mammals, river otters do emerge during the day in areas undisturbed by humans. The best time to look for these creatures is between dusk and dawn.

North America. With webbed paws, a waterproof coat, and special flaps over its nose and ears, it is well adapted to life in the water. This animal dives underwater for several minutes at a time to hunt for fishes, frogs, and large insects.

CHAPTER 4

From Stream's Head to River's Mouth: Who Lives Where and Why?

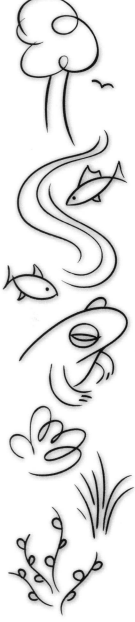

IN 1977, A YOUNG ENGLISHMAN SET out on an unusual journey through the United States. He traveled 6,130 kilometers (3,810 miles) through thirteen states— not by car or air, but by water. In a 16-foot, one-man kayak, Niles Francis paddled from the **headwaters** of the Missouri River to the mouth of the Mississippi, following the water's path to the ocean.

Such a journey reveals a constantly changing panorama of stream features and habitats. The boulder-strewn mountain brook gives way to the pools and riffles of the gravel-bottomed stream, which leads to the sand- or mud-bottomed rolling river. Current velocity seems to decrease while the volume of water increases. The temperature of the shaded, snow-fed mountain water rises as it moves to the open expanse of the lowland river.

As the physical features change, so do the animals and plants. Trout, common in cool mountain streams, are replaced by bass and sunfish. Later catfish and carp predominate. The dipper of the mountains and the kingfisher of the forest give way to the eagle and osprey of the river. The algae and mosses of the mountain brook are succeeded by the plankton and aquatic plants of the river.

Why do trout live in mountain streams but never in rivers? Why is the dipper never seen perched on a riverbank? To answer these questions, stream biologists study the physical and chemical features of rivers and streams. Stream features such as temperature, light, current velocity, type of channel bottom or substrate, **pH** levels, and oxygen all play major roles in determining the distribution of stream plants and animals.

Living things require specific conditions to survive and grow. If any of these conditions are not met, the organism's survival is threatened. These conditions are called limiting factors.

In this chapter, you'll play the role of a scientist, investigating how environmental factors determine where certain creatures live. Don't be afraid to modify the following activities so that they are more appropriate for your situation. Be creative and have fun! That's what science is all about.

PROJECT 14

Taking a Stream's Temperature

Measuring a stream's temperature can be as easy as sticking a thermometer in a beaker of water. But try measuring water temperature at a specific depth in a fast-flowing stream and you may run into problems. This activity describes a method for measuring stream temperatures at the water's

surface and at specific depths, using a simple device to cir-
cumvent the effects of the current. You'll need a thermometer; 3 meters (10 ft.) of string; a measuring tape; a
waterproof marker; a saw; some tape (or pieces of fabric);
some perforated PVC piping (look for 3- or 4-inch-diameter
perforated piping at home-supply stores); your journal; a pencil; and some graph paper (optional).

You can buy a thermometer encased in plastic or metal,
but an ordinary thermometer borrowed from your school science lab will work just as well. Pool-supply stores and pet
stores also sell thermometers. ***Don't use mercury thermometers! If they break, these thermometers leak mercury, which is toxic to you and to the stream creatures.***

Before you take a stream's temperature, begin by measuring the air temperature. Make sure the thermometer bulb
is clean, dry, and out of the direct sun as you take a reading.
In your journal, record the air temperature, time, percent
cloud cover, and type of precipitation, if any.

To measure surface water temperature, hold the thermometer by a string just under the water surface for several
minutes. Record the temperature in your journal.

Do you want to know the temperature of that cold spot
at your favorite swimming hole? To measure it, set up a well.
Cut one end of the PVC piping at a slant so that it can easily
be pushed into the streambed. Select a site in a deep pool
where your well won't be disturbed. Tie a piece of flagging to
a tree branch to mark the site.

To use this device, you'll need a thermometer tied to a 3-
meter (10-ft.) piece of string marked every 50 centimeters
(20 in.). (Use a waterproof marker.) The distances should be
measured from the bulb of the thermometer. Lower the thermometer into the well, noting the depth on the string. Allow
the thermometer to adjust for a few minutes, then rapidly
raise it to the surface. Read the temperature and record it
in your journal. Take the water temperature at the surface
and at 50-centimeter (20-in.) intervals from the surface to
the streambed. Is there much change in temperature with increasing depth?

Compare water temperatures (at the same depth) in shady and sunny stream stretches. How much does the stream temperature change over a 24-hour cycle? What are the high and low temperatures in the winter, summer, spring, and fall? How closely does the water temperature follow the changes in air temperature? Use the graph paper to plot the changes in air and water temperature over several months.

✔ Doing More

Compare temperatures in shallow backwaters and shallow riffles over the course of a day. Is the temperature change similar or different in these two areas?

Locate a river that has been dammed. Compare water temperatures above and below the dam. Is water released from the top of the dam or from the bottom? How might this affect downstream water temperature?

INVESTIGATION **9**

Too Hot, Too Cold, Just Right: Temperature and Distribution of Stream Fishes

Rainbow trout prefer cold water, sticklebacks like cool waters, and largemouth bass live in warmer waters. The desert pupfish lives in water that may get as warm as 40 to 45°C. That's more than 100°F! Stream temperature affects the growth, reproduction, development, and life cycle of stream creatures including fishes. Each species is adapted to thrive within a specific range of temperatures. Temperature also affects the amount of dissolved oxygen in the water.

Try exploring the distribution of fishes along several kilometers of a small stream. Does stream temperature change along that stretch? Do the changes in temperature explain the distribution of fishes? To answer that question, you'll need a topographic map; a thermometer; some string; a highlighter; a field guide to the freshwater fishes; some flagging tape (or pieces of fabric); and a waterproof marker. Once you've selected a method to survey stream fishes (see Project 10), collect the gear you'll need. Make sure your fishing license and any necessary permits are up-to-date and be sure to bring along a group of friends.

Spread the map out and look for a 10-kilometer (6-mi.) section of a small stream. Try to find a stretch that includes an inflow from a spring, lake, or reservoir. Once you have chosen a section, highlight it on the map. Use a piece of string and the bar scale at the bottom of the map to divide the waterway into 1-kilometer (0.6 mi.) sections.

Now study the stream stretch to select sites for your surveys. Look for places with easy access, such as road crossings, bridges, and canoe launches. The number of sites you choose depends on the amount of time and the number of people available. Select five to ten sites, evenly spaced along the stream section. Number the sites in a downstream direction. If any are on private land, be sure to ask the landowner for permission to access the land.

Plan to visit all the sites over a 1- to 2-week period at about the same time each day. Take your fishing gear, a thermometer, some flagging, a marker, binoculars, and a fish identification guide with you to each station.

Once you reach a site, tie a piece of flagging to a tree branch and mark the station number on the flagging. Record the air temperature, and then check the stream temperature by holding the thermometer about 5 centimeters (2 in.) under the water surface for several minutes (see Project 14).

Use the same survey method at each station. Record the species present and the numbers of each species you collect as shown in Table 5 on the next page. Remember to keep your hands wet if you handle a fish directly, and return the fishes to the stream unharmed.

Can you explain the distribution of fish species in terms of temperature preferences? Can you think of other explanations for the observed distribution (Hint: food availability, pH, current velocity, dissolved oxygen levels)?

Table 5 Temperature and Distribution of Fishes			
Site	Air Temperature	Stream Temperature	Fish Species
1	20°C	15°C	brook trout
2	20°C	17°C	brook trout, black-nosed dace

✔ Doing More

Stream temperature may limit the distribution of other stream creatures. Try collecting data on stream temperature and the distribution of species of stream invertebrates along a small stream using a kick net (see Appendix and Project 6 for instructions on constructing and using a kick net).

INVESTIGATION 10

How To Use A Secchi Disk

Plants and algae need light to grow. Because light penetrating the water is absorbed by the water as well as by suspended materials, the amount of light present decreases with water depth. How deep can stream plants live and still have enough light? To measure the amount of light available at different depths, scientists use a light meter. You can make approximate estimates using a simple black-and-white disk called a **Secchi disk,** named for its inventor, an eighteenth-century Italian oceanographer (see Appendix to learn how to make your own Secchi disk).

Gather a Secchi disk and two spring-loaded clothespins. Select a river or a deep quiet pool in a stream and visit it around midday. From a dock, boat, or the bank, slowly lower the Secchi disk into the water and watch it descend. Work from a tree-shaded area or the shaded side of the boat or dock to get the clearest view of the disk. Mark the depth at which you can no longer see the disk by clipping a clothespin to the rope at the waterline.Slowly lower the disk another 1 meter (3 ft.), then begin raising it. Observe its ascent and clip a second clothespin to the line when the disk reappears. Fold the rope between the two clothespins in half and measure the distance from the fold to the disk. This distance is the average Secchi depth for that site.

Repeat the procedure at a few other sites along the river or stream. Try to replicate the conditions of the first trial. The weather, the position of the sun, and roughness of the water can all affect Secchi disk readings. Note these conditions in your journal.

The reading is the lowest depth at which sufficient light reflects off the Secchi disk for you to see it. Most readings will be in the range of 2 to 10 meters (6 to 30 ft.) Do you think plants can live deeper than this? For a rough approximation of the lowest depth at which plants can live, multiply your Secchi depth reading by two. Better yet, try Investigation 11!

✔ **Doing More**

Use your Secchi disk to monitor the clarity of a local stream or river. Take monthly readings over a year. A change in the Secchi depth may indicate a change in the health of the waterway. For example, an increase in surface runoff due to road construction or clear-cutting in the watershed will cloud the waterway with soil that is washed downstream, and that can affect Secchi depth readings.

Way Down Deep: Light, Depth, and Algae

Do you like working puzzles? Do you think you're pretty good at solving problems? That is what scientists do every day. Here's a colossal puzzle for you: Why does the rainbow trout live where it does and not somewhere else? Questions about the distribution of plants and animals across Earth's surface are central to the science of ecology and have perplexed and intrigued scientists for centuries.

Try your hand at science sleuthing with the activity described here. Your mission is to investigate an environmental factor—light—to find out how it might control where the attached algae of streams and rivers is found. Here's what you need to know: (1) Algae need light to grow; (2) the amount of light decreases with stream depth; and (3) algae will grow on an acrylic sheet left in a stream for several weeks.

Should you choose to accept this assignment, you'll need your footgear and an acrylic vertical sampler (see Appendix for a diagram and instructions for building a vertical sampler). Choose a clear, sunlit stream with deep pools and riffles, and little if any shading from nearby trees. Make sure attached algae or periphyton are present (see Project 13). Plan on making an initial trip to set up the experiment and then several more trips over a 5- to 10-week period to observe and measure the algal growth.

Ready to begin the experiment? Grab your footgear, some cording, a hammer and stakes, some bricks, and the sampler. On your first trip to the stream, survey it for deep pools. Working from the stream bank, take a depth mea-

Freshwater algae, growing attached to hard surfaces in a stream bed (periphyton), or floating in the current (plankton), form the basis of many stream food chains.

surement of a pool using a weighted rope marked every 50 centimeters (20 in.).

Before placing the sampler in the pool, look for a good place to tie the upper end of it. A fallen tree or overhanging branch works well, or string some rope between stakes hammered into each side of the stream bank and attach the sampler to the rope.

Holding the top rope of the sampler, drop the sampler and the bricks into the stream. Let the current pull the acrylic strip downstream while you hold the upper end (see Appendix). Try to position the sampler so that it moves as little as possible in the stream. *Be careful in deep water! Work from the bank with the help of a friend.* Tie the top rope to a support so that the sampler stays in position. Leave the sampler in the stream for 5 to 10 weeks; check on it weekly or biweekly.

To find out how much algae is growing along the length of sampler, you'll need to measure **biomass** per unit area. Biomass is the total weight of all the organisms in a specific area. Before you retrieve the sampler, number and weigh ten aluminum weighing dishes. Record the data in Table 6 (the Dry Mass Data Sheet).

Return to the stream with a razor blade, a waterproof marker, a measuring stick, the weighing dishes, a copy of the dry mass data sheet, your journal, and a pencil. Mark the waterline on the vertical sampler after you pull it from the stream. Working on the stream bank, scrape the algae from each square with a razor blade and carefully place the sample in a preweighed aluminum dish. Combine the scrapings from three adjacent squares into one dish.

Before leaving the stream, measure the depth of each group of three squares from the waterline to the center of the group.

Return home or to your school science lab to dry your samples. When the sample weights no longer decrease with continued drying, reweigh the samples. Calculate the dry mass of each sample by subtracting the weight of the empty weighing dish from the total weight. To determine where

Table 6 Dry Mass Data Sheet (for Use with Vertical Sampler)

Weigh Dish No.	Weight of Weigh Dish (mg) A	Dish + Dry Sample B	Dry Mass (mg) B – A	Dry Mass/ Unit Area (mg/cm²)	Square No. on Vertical Sampler	Average Sample Depth (cm)

algae grew best along the length of the vertical sampler, calculate the dry mass/unit area of each sample; divide the dry
mass by the area of the sampler scraped ($300 \ cm^2$).

What do your results tell you? Does light seem to limit
algae growth at increasing depth? Can you think of other factors that might also affect algae distribution (Hint: did you observe any snails or other grazers on the acrylic sheet or in
the stream?)? To complicate matters, remember that periphyton includes some creatures that don't rely on light to
make their food so they may not be limited by light levels. How
might this fact affect your results?

✔ Doing More

Set up a vertical sampler in both a riffle and a pool to compare the attached algae biomass at the same depths. What
factors could account for any differences you might find (Hint:
see Investigation 2)?

CHAPTER 5

Brown Leaves and Green Algae: The Flow of Energy

ON A CRISP, CLEAR AUTUMN DAY, A leaf caught in a gust of wind twirls slowly and lands on the surface of a small woodland stream. It floats downstream until, suddenly, it is pinned against a rock by the current.

A succession of creatures begin to attack the leaf. Bacteria and fungi are the first to colonize the leaf surface, dining on the small molecules that leach from the leaf, and then on the leaf itself.

In the weeks and months that follow, a wide variety of other stream critters join the feast. Stonefly **nymphs,** caddisfly larvae, and crane fly larvae graze on the softer parts of the leaf, along with small, shrimplike **crustaceans** called amphipods. The leftovers are washed downstream to serve as a snack for other stream animals.

A top predator in many aquatic food chains, ospreys feed almost exclusively on fish.

Leaves are an important source of en-ergy and nutri-ents for the communities of woodland streams. But not all streams rely on food falling in; some are driven by the light of the sun. Aquatic plants and algae capture the energy from light and use it to grow and reproduce. Other stream inhabitants graze on the algae and plants, and these creatures, in turn, become food for predators.

The feeding relationships in an environment can be described by a **food chain** or a **food web** (see Figure 16). As one animal eats another, energy and nutrients are transferred. The **producers**—plants and algae—are first in the chain of events. **Consumers**—including larger mi-croscopic creatures, invertebrates, and vertebrates—feed directly or indirectly on the producers. Some consume plant material, others eat herbivores or other consumers. A special group of consumers feeds on nonliving mater-

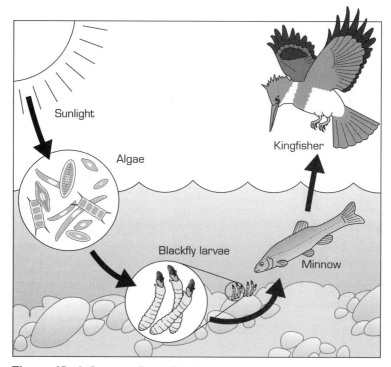

Figure 16 A Stream Food Chain

ial like leaf litter, wood debris, and the feces of stream animals.

To better understand all the feeding relationships in a stream, stream scientists categorize invertebrates according to how they obtain their food. Invertebrates may be shredders, filtering collectors, gathering collectors, scrapers, or predators. When monitored over time, changes in the relative abundance of these groups can indicate a change in the health of the stream.

In this chapter you will have the opportunity to investigate the feeding relationships in a nearby stream in a variety of ways. You can construct leaf packs and watch the creatures that come to dine; examine the stomach contents of the fishes in your stream to figure out what they eat; and survey the invertebrate population to determine the food base in your stream.

Leaf Packs and Colonizers

How does a brown-leaf sandwich drenched with bacteria and fungi sound to you? Not too good? To many stream invertebrates, it's a gourmet feast. To see what creatures you can lure with such enticing fare, try setting leaf packs in a shallow woodland stream (see Figure 17).

You'll need your footgear; a small garbage bag; some 15-pound test, monofilament fishing line; a heavy-duty sewing needle; twenty large coat buttons; a waterproof marker; ten waterproof tags; ten bricks; a thermometer; an aquatic net; ten resealable plastic bags; a hand lens; forceps; a field guide to aquatic invertebrates; a field guide to trees and shrubs; your journal; and a pencil.

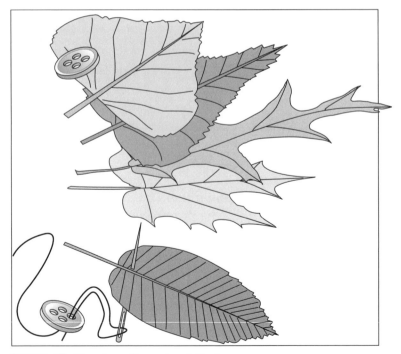

Figure 17 Constructing a Leaf Pack

Select a wadeable stream with lots of trees or shrubs along its banks. Plan on making an initial trip to the stream to collect leaves, a second trip to set up the experiment, and several additional trips to examine the leaf packs.

During your first visit to the stream, take a short walk and note the types and abundance of trees along the stream bank. Use your field guide to help you identify the trees or shrubs. Within the stream, look for clumps of leaves caught against rocks or fallen trees. Now return to the stream bank and collect about 200 green leaves from the dominant trees and shrubs and store them in a garbage bag.

At home, air-dry the leaves until they are completely dry (at least a week). Divide the leaves into ten equal batches. Soak each batch in hot water for 5 to 10 minutes to soften the leaves. With a heavy-duty sewing needle and some fishing line, sew each group of leaves together to form a moderately loose pack. Run the needle and fishing line through the **petiole** or midvein of each leaf and then through a large button placed at the top and bottom of each pack. Later, you'll fasten the packs to a brick, so leave some extra line attached to the pack. Assign a number to each pack and tag it with a waterproof tag.

At the stream site, fasten each pack to the face of a brick. To mimic the natural placement of leaves caught in a stream, position each brick so that the leaf pack is pushed up against it by the current. Sketch a rough map of the stream section in your journal and mark the sites of the leaf packs.

Monitor the leaf packs weekly in the spring and summer when stream temperatures range from 20 to 30°C (68 to 86°F) or monthly in the fall and winter, when stream temperatures might fall to between 0 and 20°C (32 and 68°F). At each visit, be sure to check and record the water temperature. Then retrieve a pack from the stream by scooping it up with an aquatic net. Seal the leaves in plastic bags to transport them home.

Back in your school lab or at home, look for living creatures and changes in the leaves. Use a hand lens or ask your science teacher if you can use a **dissecting microscope**. With either of these devices you'll be able to see a number of invertebrates including insect larvae and crustaceans. Algae, strands of fungal **hyphae,** bacteria, and **protozoans** may be visible with a compound microscope. A field guide will help you identify your finds.

Which parts of the leaves seem to be preferred by the animal community? Which creatures appear first on the leaves? Can you tell which animals are eating the leaves and which are simply attaching themselves to the leaves?

✔ Doing More

To determine the rate of leaf material loss due to animal activity, stuff several plastic sandwich bags with dried leaves until they are all the same weight. (You can use a laboratory, kitchen, or postal scale.) Construct leaf packs, and place them in the stream as described above.

Retrieve a pack after 24 hours, and then weekly or monthly depending on the water temperature. Carefully wash the leaves. Dry them at room temperature or at a low oven setting (150°F). Weigh the dried leaves. To calculate percent loss per day, use the following formulas. Note that the initial weight is taken from the pack retrieved after 24 hours.

$$\text{Percent remaining} = \frac{\text{Weight}_{final}}{\text{Weight}_{initial}} \times 100$$

$$\text{Percent loss per day} = \frac{(100 - \text{percent remaining})}{\text{Number of days leaves were in stream}}$$

Compare processing rates in different stream habitats or stream orders. Try using leaf packs made from a single type of leaf. Can you detect any food preferences in your invertebrate diners? Which leaf types are consumed fastest or slowest?

What Do Fishes Eat?

What did you have for dinner last night? If you ate fish, you were the final link in an aquatic food chain. To figure out the rest of the chain, you'll need to know what the fish ate.

While you may not be able to observe a fish feeding first-hand, you can look at the end result by examining its stomach contents. You'll need some freshly caught fishes; a measuring tape; a student dissection kit (including a blunt dissection probe, scissors, a scalpel, and forceps); a hand lens or a dissecting microscope; a pipette or medicine dropper; a shallow white tray; a pair of cotton work gloves; and a dissection tray (a large cookie sheet or cafeteria tray will work well).

If you plan on catching your own fish, make sure your fishing license is current. Pick a time when your favorite fish might be feeding to ensure that the stomach contents you examine are fresh. You may want to begin your study by using

This largemouth bass chasing a prey, could in turn be dinner for a river otter or a person with a fishing pole.

only the largest fishes you catch: keep those that measure 20 centimeters (8 in.) or longer (from snout to the base of the tail). The stomachs are more easily identified in larger fishes.

Kill the fish by hitting its head against a hard surface. To expose the stomach, grab the fish along its back and turn it upside down. Make a shallow incision from the **anus** (or vent) to the gill area, using a scalpel or sharp scissors. Turn the fish on its side and continue to cut up the sides and across the back. Expose the internal organs by lifting away the cut-out area of skin.

You'll see a number of organs including the heart, kidney, liver, stomach, and intestines (see Figure 18). To find the stomach, insert a blunt dissection probe through the mouth or anus until you reach the stomach, a sacklike part of the digestive tract (the intestines are usually much thinner and coiled). Near the juncture of the stomach and intestines you may see some short fingerlike projections, called **caeca.**

Cut out the stomach and lay it on the white tray. With a scissors or scalpel, open up the stomach and flush out its

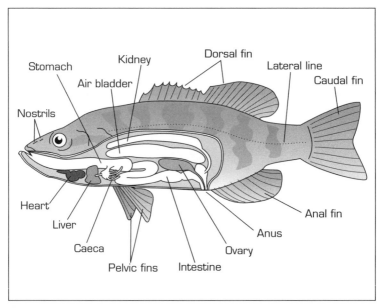

Figure 18 Anatomy of a Fish

contents with a squirt of water from a pipette or medicine dropper.

With a hand lens or dissecting microscope, examine the stomach contents. What do you see? Don't be discouraged if you can't identify everything. Try to separate the material into major groups. Do you see any plant material? Are there any insects in the stomach contents? Are they aquatic or terrestrial? Do you see any worms? Compare the stomach contents of different fish species or different individuals of the same species.

✔ Doing More

If you'd rather not kill a fish to examine what's in its stomach, try making a stomach pump to flush out the stomach contents without harming the fish (see Figure 19). The pump can be made from a spray bottle with a squeeze handle and adjustable nozzle; some aquarium tubing measuring 10 to 15

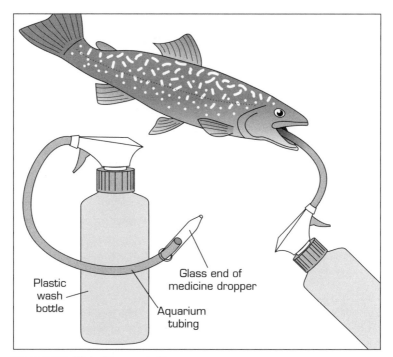

Plastic wash bottle

Glass end of medicine dropper

Aquarium tubing

Figure 19 Fish Stomach Pump

centimeters (4 to 6 in.); and a medicine dropper. Use this pump on fishes at least 20 centimeters (8 in.) long, such as trout. You'll also need the assistance of a friend.

Fill the spray bottle with water and place one end of the plastic tubing over the nozzle (you may have to remove the cap of the nozzle in order for the tubing to fit over it). Remove the bulb of a medicine dropper and attach the other end of the tubing to the medicine dropper in the bulb's place.

Wearing wet cotton gloves, firmly grasp the fish with both hands, and hold its mouth over a shallow white tray. Have a friend push the medicine dropper with the attached plastic tubing through the fish's mouth and down into the digestive tract until some resistance is felt. Then squeeze the handle of the spray bottle to flush out the stomach contents.

Invertebrate Diners: An Analysis of Functional Feeding Groups*

Most animals have to work to get their food, and stream creatures are no exception. Some are scrapers that remove the algae covering stones and other hard surfaces. Shredders tear apart dead plant parts, such as leaf litter and wood that fall into the stream. Filtering collectors spin nets or use specialized body parts to filter small food particles from the flowing water. Gathering collectors browse the streambed for bits and pieces of food that have fallen from above. Members of the fifth feeding group, the predators, stalk or ambush unwary creatures.

How many members of each type of feeding group do you have in your stream? To investigate, you'll need a D-frame

* Modified from Cummins, Kenneth W. and Margaret A. Wilzbach, *Field Procedures for Analysis of Functional Feeding Groups of Stream Macroinvertebrates,* University of Maryland, 1985.

aquatic net (see Appendix for instructions to construct one); a hacksaw; white shallow trays and white ice-cube trays for sorting; a waterproof marker; forceps; a squirt bottle; a field guide to stream invertebrates; a pictorial key (see Figure 20 on pages 94–95); a data sheet for functional feeding group analysis (see Table 7 on page 96); and a kick net (or sieve box constructed of window screening tacked to a wood frame).

Choose a shallow wadeable stream close to home. The best time of the year for this activity is mid to late summer or midwinter to early spring, when insect populations are at their peak. When you reach the stream, look for these special stream habitats: packs of leaves; pine needles or small twigs; fallen logs or tree trunks; aquatic plant beds; cobble or gravel streambed; and a muddy or silty streambed.

From each habitat, collect the following materials using the aquatic net or a hacksaw when necessary: a handful of leaf litter from a riffle; a 15- to 25-centimeter (6- to 10-in.) section of soft wood; a scoopful of mud or silt from the top 2 to 3 centimeters (1 in.) of the streambed in a pool or backwater; one or two stones 15 to 18 centimeters (6 to 7 in.) in diameter from a riffle; and a generous handful of rooted plants or aquatic moss.

Process each sample by washing it onto a sieve (1-millimeter or $\frac{1}{16}$-in. mesh size) or a kick net. Using a squirt bottle filled with stream water, rinse the material from the screening into a white shallow tray. Label the compartments of several ice cube trays with the following abbreviations for the functional feeding groups: SHR (shredders); SCR (scrapers); CL (collectors); P (predators). (In this exercise, gathering collectors and filtering collectors are combined into one group—collectors). Referring to the pictorial key, sort the creatures into appropriate compartments. The pictorial key is designed to classify the most common stream insects; you may not be able to classify some of the invertebrates you find using this key alone. Refer to a field guide for help in classifying such creatures. Count the kinds of invertebrates and numbers of each kind for each feeding group in each habitat. Record the information on your data sheet.

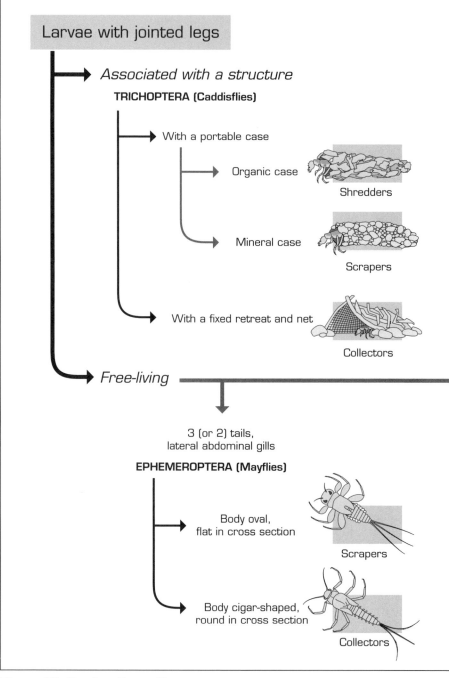

Figure 20 Feeding Group Key

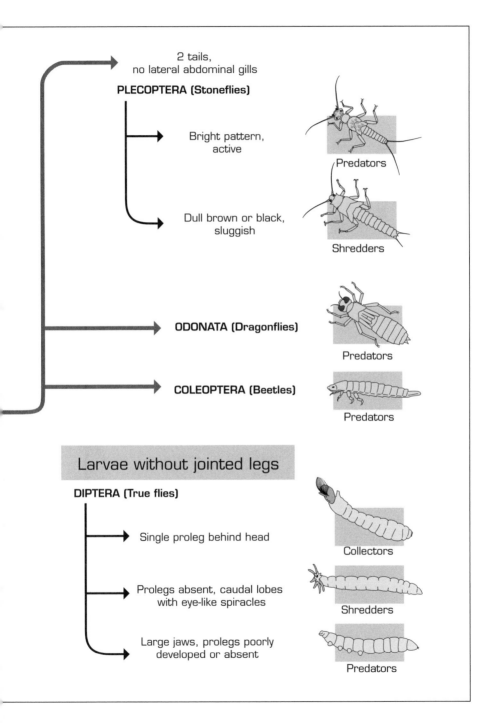

2 tails,
no lateral abdominal gills

PLECOPTERA (Stoneflies)

Bright pattern,
active

Predators

Dull brown or black,
sluggish

Shredders

ODONATA (Dragonflies)

Predators

COLEOPTERA (Beetles)

Predators

Larvae without jointed legs

DIPTERA (True flies)

Single proleg behind head

Collectors

Prolegs absent, caudal lobes
with eye-like spiracles

Shredders

Large jaws, prolegs poorly
developed or absent

Predators

Table 7 Data Sheet for Analysis of Functional Feeding Groups

Habitat Type	Stream Invertebrate Functional Feeding Groups					Totals
	Number and Kinds of Shredders (SHR)	Number and Kinds of Scrapers (SCR)	Number and Kinds of Filtering collectors (FC)	Number and Kinds of Gathering collectors (GC)	Number and Kinds of Predators (P)	
Leaf litter						
Wood						
Rocks						
Silt, mud, sand						
Large aquatic plants						

Finish your analysis by calculating, for each habitat type, the percentage that each functional feeding group represents of the total number of stream invertebrates collected. Can you present your data using a bar graph or a pie chart?

Which habitat had the greatest diversity (or greatest number of different invertebrates)? Which had the least diversity?

✔ Doing More

An analysis of functional feeding groups can tell you something about the sources of energy and nutrients for a particular stream ecosystem. Can you predict which feeding groups might predominate in each of the following stream types: a second-order woodland stream with a lot of shading; a second-order meadow stream; a seventh-order stream (river) in flat, lowland country?

Monitor functional feeding groups in a neighborhood creek throughout the year. Did you see a change in the proportions of functional feeding groups during the year? (Hint: did the fall bring an increase in shredders? Or did the summer bring an increase in scrapers?)

CHAPTER 6

Muddy Waters and Slimy Stuff: The Pollution of Rivers and Streams

A HIKER WALKED WEARILY ALONG A path, pausing before beginning her mountain ascent. Beads of sweat covered her forehead. She had started her trek early that morning but by this time in the afternoon the August heat was almost unbearable. She was alone in the forest; the silence was broken only by the occasional hum of traffic in the distance. The hiker reached for her canteen, hoping for just one more swallow of water. It was empty. She looked around, shrugged her shoulders, turned off the path and walked to the edge of a small stream. Cupping her hands, she lifted the water to her lips and began to drink.

What's wrong with this scenario? It isn't safe to drink untreated water. Although the water may appear clean, few if any of the rivers and streams in the United States have remained untouched by water pollution.

We usually think of water pollution in terms of how it affects human populations. Scientists, however, define it as any disturbance to the watershed or waterway that impacts stream life. Pollutants can be chemical, biological (such as the disease-producing bacteria in fecal waste), or thermal (like the heated water released by power plants).

Pollutants are also classified according to the way they enter a body of water. **Point-source pollutants** are released from a single source such as a pipe. **Nonpoint-source pollutants** enter a waterway from widespread sources that often affect a large portion of the watershed. For example, surface runoff from rain and snowmelt carries pollutants such as pesticides and herbicides from the watershed to the drainage system. Although point-source pollution is easier to see, more damage has been done to our rivers and streams by nonpoint-source pollutants.

How healthy is the creek or stream near your home? What can you do to clean up America's streams and rivers? The activities in this chapter will help you answer these questions.

Remember to follow the water safety rules when working at a stream site (see Introduction). If the stream appears discolored or has an odor, wear rubber gloves to protect your hands and arms. Keep your hands away from your face and wash up when you're finished.

~~~~~~~~~~~~~~~~~~~~~~~~~~~~

INVESTIGATION 15

How Clean Is Your Stream?

Although you could do a battery of chemical tests to give the stream near your home a checkup, there is a less expensive and simpler method—survey the stream invertebrates. Some stream insects tolerate polluted waters well, while others are extremely sensitive and unable to survive. By using these stream inhabitants as indicators, you can readily assess the health of your stream.

Collect your footgear; a white bucket; a kick net (see the Appendix for instructions to build a kick net, or use a kitchen sieve lined with cheesecloth); forceps; some white plastic trays; a hand lens; and some collecting jars. You'll also need a field guide to aquatic invertebrates.

Before you go, use your field guide to study the stonefly nymphs, mayfly nymphs, and caddisfly larvae (or see Figure 12 on pages 48–49). These aquatic insects are very sensitive to water pollution. Their presence or absence can be an important indicator of stream-water quality.

Mayfly nymphs looks like flattened roaches with three (or sometimes two) hairlike tails, a series of gills along the sides of their abdomens, and six jointed legs. Stonefly nymphs are similar in appearance. They can be distinguished from mayflies by their double-clawed feet, smooth abdomen (no gills), and two hairlike tails.

Caddisflies are caterpillarlike creatures that build their own mobile homes (or cases) from sand, rocks, twigs, or leaves. They have six jointed legs and two fleshy lobes that protrude from their back end; each lobe has a single hook or claw.

Now that you are acquainted with a few of the stream residents, gather your equipment and head to a gravel-bed stream with riffles and pools. Walk along the bank and look for a riffle to study.

Once you've selected a riffle, pick up a stone at least 15 centimeters (6 in.) in diameter and quickly place it into a bucket filled with stream water. While the rock is immersed in the bucket, rub the entire surface to dislodge any stream creatures. When the stone is clean, return it to the streambed. Process several more large rocks in the same manner.

Filter the water in the bucket by pouring it through a kick net or a kitchen sieve lined with cheesecloth. Transfer the animals collected to a white tray containing a small amount of stream water. Examine your catch for mayflies, stoneflies, and caddisflies.

Label three collecting jars with these group names. Place the mayflies, stoneflies, and caddisflies you have collected in the appropriate jar.

If your stream is severely polluted, you probably won't see any stoneflies, mayflies, or caddisflies. If it's moderately polluted, the stream will probably have one but not all of these insects. If stoneflies, mayflies, and caddisflies are all present, the water quality is probably good to excellent. For a method of monitoring sand- or mud-bottomed rivers or streams, contact the Izaak Walton League of America (see the For Further Information section at the back of this book).

✔ Doing More

For a more thorough evaluation of your stream's health, try the following procedure. Additional information can be provided by the Izaak Walton League of America, the Adopt-A-Stream Foundation, the United States Environmental Protection Agency, as well as other environmental organizations (see the section headed For Further Information at the back of this book).

Using a kick net, sample a 1-meter^2 (1-sq. yd.) area of a riffle. Carry the kick net to the stream bank and sort through your catch using a hand lens, some white plastic trays, white ice-cube trays, and a field guide. Refer to the Stream Quality Rating Data Sheet on pages 102–103 for a list of animals you may find in your stream.

Completing Table 8 will help you rate the water quality in your stream. Sample two more 1-meter^2 (1-sq. yd.) areas to obtain two additional ratings, each based on a single sample. Base your stream's final water-quality rating on the highest value of the three samples.

Table 8 Stream Quality Rating Data Sheet

Pollution Sensitivity	Name of Organism or Group	Present in stream (X = yes; 0 = no)	Weighting Factor	Index Values (number of X's times weighting factor)
pollution sensitive	caddisfly larvae		3	
	dobsonfly larvae (hellgrammite)			
	mayfly nymphs			
	snails (gilled)			
	stonefly nymphs			
	water penny			
	riffle beetle adult			
somewhat pollution sensitive	beetle larvae		2	
	clams			
	crane fly larvae			
	crayfish			
	damselfly nymphs			

Category	Organism	Value
	dragonfly nymphs	
	scuds (sideswimmers or amphipods)	
	sowbugs (pillbugs or isopods)	
	fishfly larvae	
	alderfly larvae	
	watersnipe fly larvae (atherix)	
pollution tolerant	aquatic worms (oligochaetes)	1
	blackfly larvae	
	leeches	
	midge larvae	
	snails (pouch)	

Total Index Value =

Use the following ranges of total index values to rate the quality of your stream: greater than 22, excellent water quality; 17–22, good water quality; 11–16, fair quality; less than 11, poor water quality.

Monitoring Stream Sediment: Using an Imhoff Cone

The biggest threat to stream life may not be the chemicals that factories dump into waterways, but the excessive sediment that smothers stream life. Try monitoring a local stream for this pollutant, using a simple cone-shaped device called an **Imhoff cone** (you can also measure sediment levels using a Secchi disk; see Investigation 10).

You can order an Imhoff cone and holding rack from one of the supply companies listed in the section headed For Further Information at the back of this book. To save money you can substitute a rubber boot for the holding rack.

Select a nearby stream to monitor. As you walk along its banks, look for signs of soil erosion, a potential source of stream sediment. Is there an area nearby where new houses are being constructed? If the stream flows through a forested area, is part of it being logged? Do you see areas where the land has been cleared right up to the stream bank? Plan on monitoring the sediment levels upstream and downstream from a few of these sites each week for several months.

To monitor sediment levels, fill the Imhoff cone with stream water, set it upright in a holding rack or boot and allow the materials to settle for 45 minutes. Hold the cone with the palms of your hands and briskly roll it back and forth a few times. Let the material settle for an additional 15 minutes. Use the markings on the side of the cone to measure the volume of settled matter per liter.

✔ Doing More

Visit a local water-treatment plant to learn how they monitor suspended solids. Check construction sites for the proper use of erosion-control devices, such as soil erosion fences. If you believe a site is not in compliance with local ordinances, visit your local environmental agency for advice. You may also notify the Adopt-A-Stream Foundation or the Izaak Walton

League of America (see the section headed For Further Information at the back of this book).

Monitor a stream during or immediately after a heavy rain, but be very careful: rising, fast-flowing water and slippery banks can be dangerous! Have an adult accompany you. Is there an increase in sediment levels? Compare sites in the same stream, or in different streams. Which sites had the greatest increase in sediment levels? Which had the least? Can you determine where the sediment is coming from?

INVESTIGATION **16**

Organizing a Stream Cleanup

Water pollution can take many forms. We seldom think of litter and garbage as a type of water pollution, but in rural and suburban areas our rivers and streams are strewn with refuse.

Has a stream or river in your area been the site of illegal dumping? Has your favorite swimming hole suddenly become someone's private garbage dump? Consider organizing a stream cleanup.

A successful stream cleanup depends on thorough planning. First select a nearby stream or river, then enlist a few of your friends or family members to help you with the project. Establish this small group as the planning committee, and pick a leader. Have several meetings to discuss what needs to be done and assign specific duties to each individual. Include the following in your discussion:

- advertising the event
- recruiting volunteer help
- obtaining permission from landowners along the stream
- locating access roads in the cleanup area
- notifying local or state environmental agencies

Signs such as this one have become commonplace across the country. People like you can reverse this trend!

- requesting donations of supplies from local merchants
- purchasing other supplies
- arranging for a local recycling center or landfill to accept the trash you collect

You should also walk along the stream to survey the extent and types of trash involved. At that time, establish the limits of your cleanup effort. Consider the length of the stream and the stream bank, and the area of the **riparian zone**—the land adjacent to the stream. Mark these boundaries with stakes or flagging. Also look for likely places to establish temporary holding areas for the collected refuse.

Here's a list of the supplies and equipment you may need: some heavy-duty trash bags; a folding table; some chairs; a first-aid kit; stakes; flagging or strips of fabric; work gloves; rakes; shovels; a rope or chain; a camera; drinking water; garbage cans or bins; wheelbarrows; several pick-up trucks and drivers; and lots of volunteer workers. It's a good idea to take along a cellular phone and a list of emergency numbers.

On the day of the cleanup, set up a folding table in a central area to serve as an organizing center for the event. Have at least one person staff that area at all times. Keep the cellular phone, a first-aid kit, and drinking water nearby. Also have some extra trash bags and other supplies. Have a sign-up sheet for the volunteers and be sure to ask for full names, addresses, and phone numbers in case of an emergency.

Give your volunteers a quick overview of the plan for the day. Describe the boundaries of the cleanup area, the types of refuse to be removed, and the location of the temporary holding areas. ***Warn them of potentially hazardous materials that might exist in the stream or on the stream bank. Review the basic water safety rules with your group.*** If you plan to separate recyclables from other trash, be sure to explain this to the volunteers. Emphasize that they should make an effort not to disturb the entire area. Conclude your talk with an upbeat reminder of the importance of this work.

Assign one member of the planning committee to be a photographer who documents the state of the stream before and after the cleanup. Another member of the committee should keep track of the amount and types of trash collected.

After the cleanup, tally the amount and types of refuse pulled from the stream. Prepare a short press release for the local newspaper (and offer your photographs). Contact the volunteers to thank them for their efforts. Plan a picnic at a local park to thank them and inform them of how much trash they actually removed! Pass around the photographs of the stream cleanup.

Do you want to do more to protect your river or stream? Become a volunteer monitor. Start your own group of stream watchdogs or get involved with an established group in your area. To find out about monitoring groups, contact a local environmental agency or the Izaak Walton League of America (see the section headed For Further Information at the back of this book).

INVESTIGATION 17

How Much Water Do You Use?

Pour yourself a glass of water and take a sip. Thousands or millions of years ago, those same water molecules may have been a refreshing drink for an Egyptian pharaoh or *a Tyrannosaurus rex!* All the water that's ever been on Earth is still here today—it just keeps being recycled.

So why are some people concerned about water conservation? Why not let the water run while you're brushing your teeth? If it's not really being used up, why bother conserving water? In spite of the paradox, clean water is in short supply and it is important to conserve it. Treating polluted water for our use is costly and not always effective. Using too much water drains streams and rivers, and causes a decline in stream plants and animals.

How much water do you use? Where do you use the most water? Estimate the amount of water you and your family use for various activities. You'll need a bucket; a 2-liter container (or a gallon milk jug); a stopwatch; your journal; a pencil; and a calculator.

Try estimating your water use by keeping a log of your daily water consumption for a week. You'll need your journal and a stopwatch. Record the type of water use. For use from a faucet (no appliance involved), use a stopwatch to monitor the flow time. For appliances or toilets, record the number of times each device is used.

At the end of the week, tally the totals for each type of water use on the Water Usage Worksheet. Add up the minutes of waterflow from faucets. Tally the number of uses of appliances or toilets.

Next, you'll need to determine faucet-flow rates and estimate the water volumes used in the appliances. Measure flow rates from a faucet or showerhead with a stopwatch, a bucket, and a 2-liter plastic bottle or a gallon milk jug. To determine the volume of the bucket, use the plastic bottle or the milk jug to fill it; keep track of how much water you need. Now turn the faucet on, adjust it to the flow rate you normally use. Position the bucket directly under the spout and time how long it takes to fill it. Calculate the flow rate by dividing the volume of the bucket by the elapsed time. For example, if your bucket holds 9.5 liters (2.5 gallons) and takes 10 seconds to fill, the flow rate from that fixture would be 9.5 liters (2.5 gallons) divided by $\frac{1}{6}$ minute, or 57 liters/minute (15 gallons/minute).

Refer to the worksheet to complete the estimate. Divide the total number of liters (or gallons) by the number of days in a week to calculate daily water use.

How much water does your family use everyday? Have each family member keep a daily water-use log for a week (see Table 9 on pages 110–111). Give them copies of the worksheet to use as daily logs. At the end of the week, total the logs and worksheets and calculate a daily per-person average. Daily residential water use in the United States ranges from 300 to 380 liters (80 to 100 gallons) per person. Based on these figures, how much does the average American use each year?

Table 9 Water Usage Worksheet

Note: The accepted unit for volume in the metric system is liters. In the United States, gallons are still commonly used. One liter equals 0.264 gallon, while 1 gallon equals 3.79 liters.

Type of Water (H$_2$O) Use	Total Minutes of Water Flow A	Flow Rate B	Total A x B C	Total Number of Uses D	Estimates of H$_2$O Consumed/ Use E	Total D x E F	Totals C or F
Dishwasher	N/A	N/A	N/A		60 liters [15 gal.]		
Handwashing (dishes)				N/A	N/A	N/A	
Washing machine	N/A	N/A	N/A		114 liters [30 gal.]		
Toilet	N/A	N/A	N/A		26 liters [5 gal.]		
Drinking water				N/A	N/A	N/A	
Cooking				N/A	N/A	N/A	
Tooth-brushing				N/A	N/A	N/A	

					Grand Total =
Face washing			N/A	N/A	N/A
Hand washing			N/A	N/A	N/A
Shaving			N/A	N/A	N/A
Bathing			N/A	N/A	N/A
Showers			N/A	N/A	N/A
Garden			N/A	N/A	N/A
Car washing			N/A	N/A	N/A
Lawn irrigation			N/A	N/A	N/A
Pool			N/A	N/A	N/A

N/A = Not applicable

✔ Doing More

Display your water-usage data as a bar graph or pie chart. How did you use the most water? Can you think of ways you and your family can conserve water? Ask the members of your family for ideas. Your local waterworks is also a good source of ideas. Try the American Water Works Association or the U.S. Environmental Protection Agency (see the section headed For Further Information at the back of this book) for brochures and information on water conservation. Conserving water is important. We need clean water running in our streams, not down our drains!

Conclusion

RUNNING WATER PLAYS MANY ROLES in its journey to the ocean. In this introduction to rivers and streams, we have explored three of these roles. First, it is an agent of geological change— running waters mold and sculpt Earth's surface. Second, as part of watersheds, rivers and streams funnel rainwater and melted snow from the land. Finally, rivers and streams are ecosystems—complex biological systems that provide habitats for an incredible array of animal and plant life.

Rivers and streams shape Earth's surface through the processes of erosion, transport, and deposition. As running water flows over the land, it erodes the surface, picking up small pieces of soil. As the water flows onward, it transports this sediment and deposits it on the streambed.

Over time, these processes can dramatically change the shape of the land. As a river or stream erodes its channel, a valley is formed. Where fast-moving water is suddenly slowed in its flow, deposits are laid down, and new land areas are created.

These areas can be as small as a sandbar or as large as half the state of Louisiana, which was formed over thousands of years by sediments from the Mississippi River.

While running waters rearrange the landscape, the land contributes more than just sediment to a river or stream. When rain falls on Earth's surface, some of the water travels overland. This surface runoff carries with it any chemicals or pollutants on the land and deposits them in the nearest body of water.

The land over which this runoff flows and the water that drains it make up a watershed. We have only recently begun to realize that the health of our rivers and streams depends on the way we treat our watersheds.

A healthy stream or river is much more than just a flowing body of clean water. It is an ecosystem with many components, each of which contributes to the health of the whole. This ecosystem includes the plants and animals that live in the stream; the velocity of the water flow; the type of streambed; the substances dissolved and carried in the water; and the trees and shrubs along the banks that shade the stream and drop their leaves and branches into it.

Many of our stream and river ecosystems are in danger today. By polluting our waterways and watersheds, manipulating channels and water flow, and otherwise changing the workings of rivers and streams, we have put them in peril. They need your help. Start with a creek, stream, or river in your area. Use the knowledge and experience you've gained from the activities and information in this book. Be part of the solution. Get involved. Make a difference.

Tools and Equipment

Without a lot of expense or expertise, you can put together a set of tools and equipment that will help you explore the fascinating world of rivers and streams.

You can discover new facts about a stream or river with some simple equipment. Listed below are some basic tools you might find useful in your explorations. A backpack or knapsack would easily accommodate these items:

- white plastic or enamel pans and white ice-cube trays for sorting small stream creatures
- a 15-centimeter (6-in.) ruler
- a magnifying glass or hand lens
- collecting vials (white drug bottles or plastic peanut-butter jars work well)
- forceps or tweezers
- a kitchen strainer
- a small aquarium net
- thermometers for air and water (see aquarium suppliers for inexpensive models)
- preserving fluid (ethanol or rubbing alcohol)
- a small pipette or clear medicine dropper

For more in-depth studies, you'll need some specialized equipment. These collecting devices can reveal an incredible array of otherwise hidden stream occupants. Try your hand at making the following equipment. Armed with these tools, you'll be ready for some exciting biological adventures!

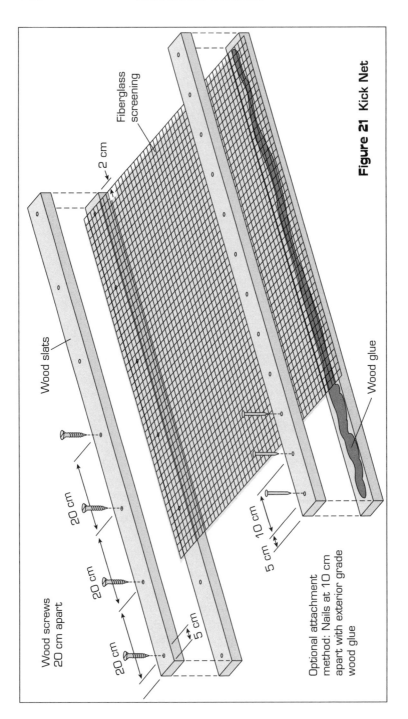

Figure 21 Kick Net

Kick Net

One of the most useful pieces of equipment for collecting insect larvae and other small animals from shallow gravel-bed streams is the kick net (see Figure 21). To make one, you'll need four 1.5 meter (5-ft.) wood slats; thirty small finishing nails and a hammer (or sixteen no. 10 1-in. flat-head wood screws and a screwdriver); a drill with a $\frac{7}{64}$-in. (3-mm) drill bit; a 1 meter-square sheet of light-gray fiberglass window screening; exterior wood glue; and scissors. The wood slats can be strips of wood molding or 1 × 2 boards (the actual dimensions are 1.9 centimeters × 3.8 centimeters [$\frac{3}{4}$ in. × $1\frac{1}{2}$ in.]. If you use wood molding, use smaller screws or nails than those listed above.

Place two wood slats parallel to each other on a hard surface (such as a paved driveway), 1 meter (39-in.) apart. Their widest surface should face down.

If you plan to use screws to hold the wood slats together, drill pilot holes every 20 centimeters (8 in.) along the center of each slat. If you are using glue and nails, coat the face of each slat with wood glue. Place a cut edge of screening along the length of each slat. Position the woven edge of screening 2.5 centimeters (1 in.) away from the top edge of each slat. Lay the second set of slats on top of the first set. Join the slats by driving the wood screws into the pilot holes. If you used glue, nail the slats together using finishing nails spaced every 10 centimeters (4 in.).

Hester-Dandy Sampler

Using nets is one way to collect stream invertebrates. If you'd rather not get your feet wet, try using a Hester-Dandy sampler. It's easy to construct (see Figure 22 on the next page) and if you leave it on the streambed for several weeks, it will attract a wide array of stream creatures.

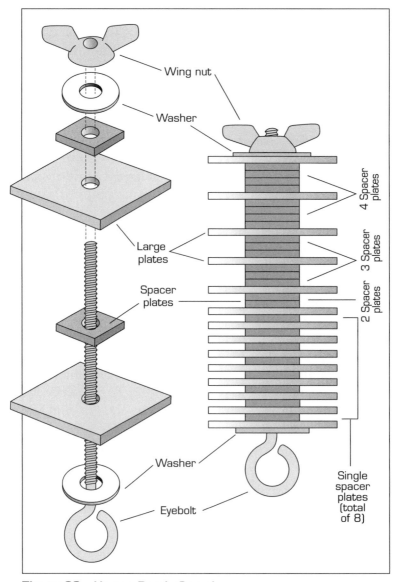

Figure 22   Hester-Dendy Sampler

The Hester-Dandy sampler consists of a series of stacked plates made from tempered hardboard. From a local hardware store, pick up a piece of $\frac{1}{8}$-inch hardboard (a trade name is Masonite) measuring at least 36 × 36 centimeters (14 × 14 in.), one $\frac{3}{16}$- × 7-inch eyebolt, two $\frac{3}{16}$-inch washers, and one wing nut to fit the eyebolt. You'll also need a drill, a $\frac{1}{4}$-inch (6-mm) drill bit, a ruler, and a table saw, band saw, or jigsaw.

Cut the hardboard into fourteen 7.5-centimeter (3-in.) squares and twenty-four 2.5-centimeter (1-in.) squares using the power saw. (Ask an adult to assist you.) With a $\frac{1}{4}$-inch drill bit, drill a central opening into each of these pieces. Holding the eyebolt in your hand, place a washer on the bolt and then begin stacking alternating large and small plates onto the eyebolt (see Figure 22). After adding the ninth large plate, place two small plates or spacers onto the bolt.

Complete the device by adding three more large plates separated by three spacers, then two large plates separated by four spacers. After the last large plate, add a washer, and screw on the wing nut.

To use the sampler, simply place it in the streambed. If the current is swift, anchor the sampler with a rope tied to a stake, weight, or tree branch. In mud-bottom channels, it's best to hang the sampler from an over-hanging tree branch or an object on the bank. Suspend the device just above the streambed.

After 2 or 3 weeks, you should have a population of stream critters living between the hardboard plates. Retrieve the sampler from the stream using a net to avoid losing your catch. To examine the creatures, take the sampler apart over a shallow white tray. Use a soft toothbrush to gently remove any animals clinging to the sampler pieces.

D-Frame Aquatic Net

To make an aquatic net that is versatile enough to sample a sandy or muddy streambed, catch unsuspecting fishes, and sweep water striders off the water surface, you'll need the following materials: 120 centimeters (4-ft.) of $\frac{3}{4}$- or 1-inch wooden doweling; a strip of heavy canvas measuring 18 × 95 centimeters (7 × 38 in.); 120 centimeters (4-ft.) of 9-gauge galvanized wire; a mesh laundry bag that is 43 centimeters (17 in.) long with a 53-centimeter (21-in.) diameter opening and a mesh size of 5 millimeters ($\frac{1}{4}$ in.) or less; two stainless-steel hose clamps ($\frac{9}{16}$- to $1\frac{1}{4}$-inch); a sewing machine or needle and thread; an iron and ironing board; a measuring tape; a marker; a utility knife; pliers; a hammer; a screwdriver; a drill and a $\frac{7}{32}$-inch drill bit. Hose clamps can be purchased at a hardware or auto-parts store. An old mop handle or broom handle can be used in place of the wooden dowel.

To make the frame, determine the exact center of the length of wire. Mark this point (see Figure 23). Bend the wire at the indicated points. Work on a flat surface, and use pliers to make the bends. Clip the free ends of the wire 1.5 centimeters ($\frac{1}{2}$ in.) from the last bend. With your hands, round the two 34-centimeter (13.5-in.) sections while bringing the two cut ends together, forming a shape like the letter D.

To attach the mesh laundry bag to the metal frame, fold the edges of the canvas strip 1 centimeter ($\frac{1}{2}$ in.) under and press with an iron. Now fold the fabric in half lengthwise, and press again. Drape the strip over the frame along the pressed fold. Sandwich the edge of the laundry-bag opening between the two pieces of canvas. Using the needle and thread, sew the canvas strip to the mesh bag.

Prepare the handle by drilling a 5-millimeter ($\frac{7}{32}$-in.) diameter hole 9 centimeters ($3\frac{1}{2}$ in.) from one end of the dowel. Rotate the dowel 180 degrees and drill a second hole 6.5 centimeters ($2\frac{1}{2}$ in.) from the same end of the dowel. With a utility knife, cut two shallow, V-shaped grooves from each hole to the end of the rod. The grooves should be just deep enough to snugly fit the wire you used for the framing. Fit the shaped net frame to the handle and drive the wire ends into the drilled openings with a hammer.

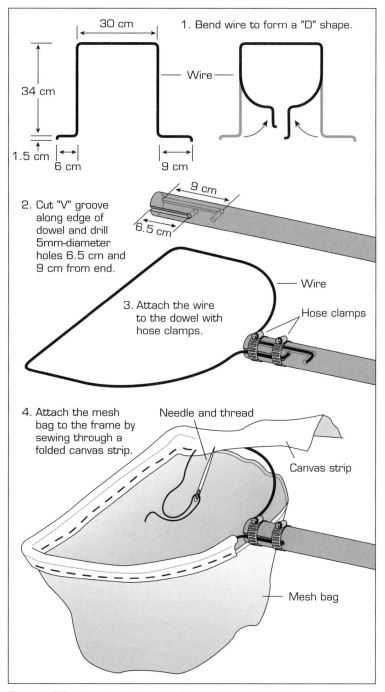

1. Bend wire to form a "D" shape.

30 cm

34 cm

Wire

1.5 cm

6 cm

9 cm

2. Cut "V" groove along edge of dowel and drill 5mm-diameter holes 6.5 cm and 9 cm from end.

9 cm

6.5 cm

Wire

3. Attach the wire to the dowel with hose clamps.

Hose clamps

4. Attach the mesh bag to the frame by sewing through a folded canvas strip.

Needle and thread

Canvas strip

Mesh bag

Figure 23 Constructing a D-Frame Aquatic Net

To secure the net frame to the doweling, slide two hose clamps over the handle as shown in Figure 23. Use a screwdriver to tighten the hose clamps.

Plankton Net

To snag some tiny stream creatures, construct a net of silk or nylon fabric (see Figure 24). You'll need a 15-centimeter (6-in.) diameter plastic embroidery hoop; scissors; a fishing swivel; three 1.5-ounce (43-g) fishing weights; 3 meters (10 ft.) of $\frac{1}{8}$-inch braided synthetic rope; and 120 centimeters (4 ft.) of 30-pound test, monofilament fishing line.

The type of fabric you choose will determine your success in netting stream or river plankton. Look for lightweight white or beige nylon or silk fabric with tightly woven threads. A fabric store or used-clothing shop are good places to begin your search. You will want a fabric with mesh openings of 0.1 millimeter (34 threads/in.). Use a hand lens or borrow a dissecting microscope from your school to determine the size of the mesh opening or the thread count. Check out small swatches of fabric before you make your final selection. You'll need about 70 centimeters ($\frac{3}{4}$ yd.) of fabric to make this plankton net.

Once you have found some suitable material, cut a piece measuring 53 × 51 centimeters (21 × 20 in.). Use a sewing machine to stitch a small hem along one 53-centimeter (21-in.) edge. Now stitch the two 51-centimeter (20-in.) edges together to form a cylinder. Attach the unhemmed end of the cylinder to the inner ring of the embroidery hoop by bringing the fabric up through the center of the hoop and folding 2 to 3 centimeters (1 in.) of material over the outer edge of the inner hoop. Tuck the cut edge of fabric back under itself and use a needle and thread to sew the folded edge to the fabric just below the hoop. Snap the outer hoop around the inner embroidery hoop. Adjust the tightening screw to hold the

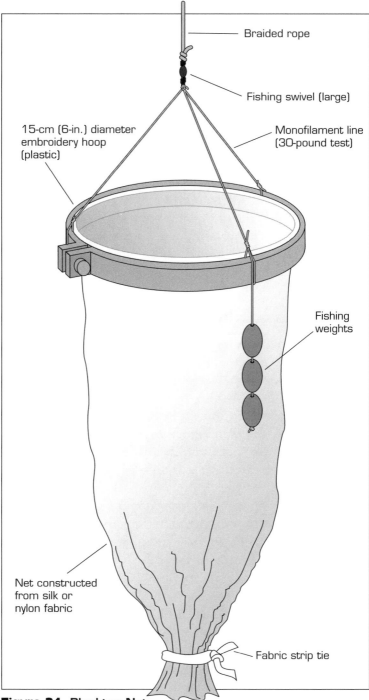

Braided rope

Fishing swivel (large)

15-cm (6-in.) diameter embroidery hoop (plastic)

Monofilament line (30-pound test)

Fishing weights

Net constructed from silk or nylon fabric

Fabric strip tie

Figure 24 Plankton Net

net in place. Tie the other end of the cylinder closed with a strip of fabric or string.

To make a harness to tow the plankton net, cut three 51-centimeter (20-in.) pieces of fishing line. Attach one end of each piece to the outer ring of the embroidery hoop; space them evenly around the ring. Tie the free end of each piece to a fishing swivel. Tie the braided rope to the other end of the swivel. When tying fishing line, be sure to make at least four knots to prevent it from coming undone.

Complete your net by adding three fishing weights to the outer hoop of the embroidery net using some fishing line. Without these weights, your net will probably bob at the surface. The weights ensure that your net will sink so that you can take a sample.

Weed Hook

A weed hook can be used to retrieve aquatic plants from slow-moving rivers and streams. To make a weed hook, you will need two metal coat hangers; a piece of metal piping (25-mm [1-in.] wide and 125-mm [5-in.] in length); one $\frac{1}{2}$-in. nut and washer; wire snips; and a short piece of rope (see Figure 25).

Take apart the coat hangers and straighten the wire. Cut each wire in half for a total of four 52-centimeter (20-in.) pieces. Fold each piece in half, and then fold 3 centimeters ($\frac{1}{4}$ in.) of each looped end back on itself. Insert the cut ends of wire through the center of the metal piping and hook the bent loops over the piping edge. Now bend the cut ends of the coat hanger towards the piping.

To complete the device, thread a washer and nut onto the rope. Secure it by tying several knots behind the nut. Thread the free end of the rope through the bottom of the weed hook, and pull it out the top. Pull the nut and washer tight against the wire pieces. Use the short rope to attach the weed hook to a longer piece of rope.

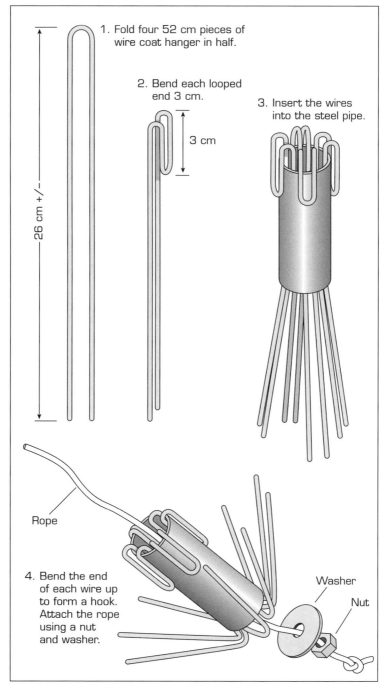

1. Fold four 52 cm pieces of wire coat hanger in half.

2. Bend each looped end 3 cm.

3 cm

26 cm +/-

3. Insert the wires into the steel pipe.

Rope

4. Bend the end of each wire up to form a hook. Attach the rope using a nut and washer.

Washer

Nut

Figure 25 Constructing a Weed Hook

Secchi Disk

A Secchi disk is a weighted black-and-white disk used to measure the clarity of standing or running water. To make your own Secchi disk, you will need the following items: a 1-gallon paint-can lid; one $\frac{5}{16}$- × 4-inch eyebolt; two $\frac{5}{16}$-inch nuts; two $\frac{5}{16}$-inch washers; three anchor-bolt washers (3 × 3 × $\frac{1}{4}$ inch); a waterproof marker; masking tape; a tape measure; a 20-meter (66-ft.) length of $\frac{1}{4}$-inch synthetic fiber rope; black and white enamel paint (spray cans or small bottles with brushes); a hammer; and a screwdriver (see Figure 26).

Wash the paint-can lid to remove any dried paint. Divide the top surface of the lid into four quadrants using a ruler and a marker. With masking tape, mask off two diagonal quadrants from each other. Paint the exposed quadrants with black glossy paint and allow them to dry. Remove the masking tape and cover the black quadrants. Paint the exposed areas white.

Once the paint is dry, use the hammer and screwdriver to punch a small hole in the center of the lid. It should be just large enough to accommodate the eyebolt. *Be sure to bend the sharp edges back (and hammer them down) after punching out the hole!* Thread a nut and then a washer onto the eyebolt. Push the eyebolt through the hole in the paint-can lid; position it so that the eye of the eyebolt is exposed to the painted side of the can lid. Add three anchor-bolt washers, one small washer, and a nut to the eyebolt. Tighten the nut so that the anchor-bolt washers fit tightly against the underside of the lid.

To make the calibrated line used to lower the disk into the water, tie a rope to the eye of the eyebolt so that the Secchi disk hangs horizontally. Using a tape measure or meter stick, measure 50 centimeters (20 in.) from the surface of the disk along the rope. Use a waterproof marker to mark this spot on the rope. Continue marking the rope every 50 centimeters (20 in.) to a final length of 20 meters (66 ft.).

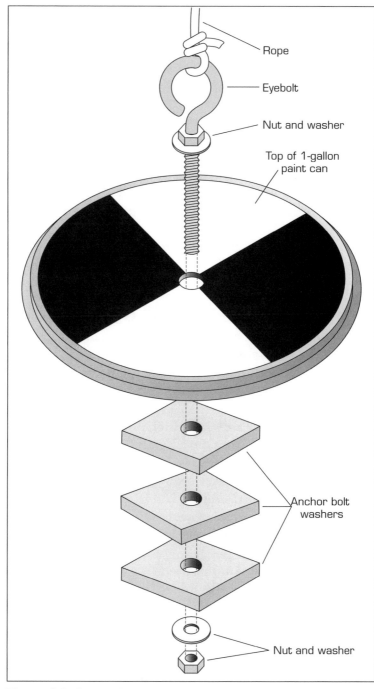

Figure 26 Secchi Disk

Vertical Sampler

To build a vertical sampler you'll need two strips of $\frac{1}{8}$-in. acrylic (Plexiglas is a trade name) measuring 15 × 130 centimeters (6 × 51 in.); four $\frac{1}{4}$- × $\frac{3}{4}$-in. bolts; four $\frac{1}{4}$-in. hex or wing nuts; two bricks; a single-edged razor blade; a weighted line measuring 5 to 10 meters (5 to 10 yd.) marked every 50 centimeters (20 in.); a drill with a $\frac{5}{16}$-in. drill bit; a screwdriver; some braided synthetic cording; two stakes; a hammer; a waterproof marker; a metric ruler; some aluminum weighing dishes; a drying oven; and a laboratory scale. Ask your science teacher how to use a laboratory scale to weigh milligram amounts of material. A glass supplier can sell you a piece of acrylic cut to the size you need. Home-supply stores also carry this material, but you may have to cut it yourself (see Figure 27).

Begin by using a waterproof marker to draw a series of 10- × 10-centimeter (4- × 4-in.) squares on both strips of acrylic. Leave an unmarked 10-centimeter (4-in.) strip at the top and bottom of each sheet. Mark the exact center of each square with a small X. Write on only one side of the acrylic.

Next, drill two series of $\frac{5}{16}$-inch holes spaced every 10 centimeters (4 in.) along the length of each strip, 1.5 centimeters (0.5 in.) from the edge. *To keep the acrylic from shattering or cracking, back the sheet with a piece of wood placed under the drilling area and drill slowly. Wear safety glasses.* At one end of each strip, drill an additional hole near a corner, 2 centimeters (1 in.) in from the top edge.

To assemble the sampler, overlap the two acrylic strips so that the marked squares line up and the drilled corner holes are at opposite ends. Screw the two plates together, using four bolts placed three squares in from each end.

Adjust the length of the vertical sampler to match the depth of the pool by removing the bolts and sliding the two strips apart. Screw the strips back together, placing

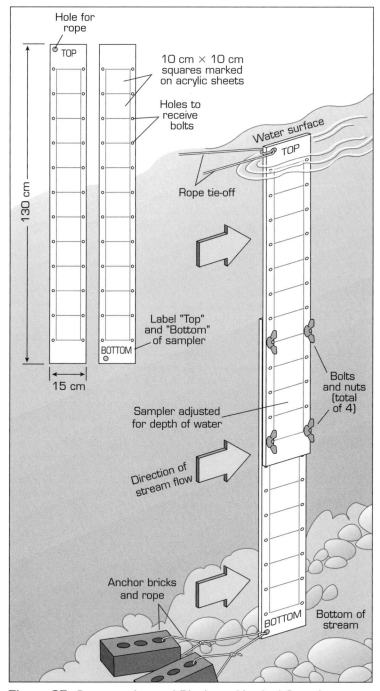

Hole for rope

TOP

10 cm × 10 cm squares marked on acrylic sheets

Holes to receive bolts

130 cm

15 cm

BOTTOM

Label "Top" and "Bottom" of sampler

Water surface

TOP

Rope tie-off

Sampler adjusted for depth of water

Direction of stream flow

Bolts and nuts (total of 4)

Anchor bricks and rope

BOTTOM

Bottom of stream

Figure 27 Constructing and Placing a Vertical Sampler

the bolts at the top and bottom of the overlapping section. With a waterproof marker, number the squares of the sampler from top to bottom.

Fold a 2-meter (80-in.) piece of cord in half and tie it to the top corner hole of the acrylic strip, pushing the looped end through the drilled hole. Thread the cut ends back through the loop, leaving two 1-meter (40-in.) sections of rope. Tie a second piece of cord to the bottom corner hole of the sampler in the same way. Attach one end of the bottom cord to a brick and pull the brick close to the sampler. Attach the second piece of bottom cord to a second brick, leaving about 50 centimeters (20 in.) between the brick and the acrylic sheet.

Glossary

algae—one-celled, photosynthetic organisms belonging to the kingdom Protista.

anus—the opening of the digestive tract through which solid waste is expelled.

arroyo—stream or stream channel in a dry environment that only fills during heavy rains.

backwater—a side channel from the main current, in which water is turned back in its course by an obstruction.

benthos—(adjective, *benthic*), the aquatic organisms that live in, on, or near the bottom of a body of water.

biomass—the weight (mass) of all the organisms of a given type in a given area.

caecum—(plural, *caeca*), a fingerlike pouching of the digestive tract in vertebrates.

channel—a hollowed-out strip of earth where a natural body of water runs or may run.

compound microscope—microscope that uses two or more lenses for forming a magnified image of a small object.

consumer—a living organism that is unable to make its food from nonliving sources, relying instead on energy stored in other living things that it eats.

contour interval—the change in elevation between contour lines on topographic maps.

contour line—lines on topographic maps that join points of equal elevation on the surface of the land above or below a reference surface.

crustaceans—a group of mostly aquatic animals belonging to the phylum Arthropoda; the group includes crab, lobster, shrimp, and crayfish as well as the lesser known microscopic forms common in plankton.

current velocity—the speed at which water in a river or stream is pulled downhill by the force of gravity. It is measured as distance traveled in a given period of time.

deposition—the process by which the products of erosion are laid down.

diatom—a type of single-celled algae that is encased in a shell composed of silica.

diatomaceous earth—a natural deposit formed from the shells of diatoms; when ground into a fine powder, it's used as an absorbent or filtering material.

dissecting microscope—or stereoscopic microscope; a microscope that provides an enlarged three-dimensional image of the object being viewed.

drainage basin—area drained by a network of streams that all flow into one main river.

drift—the material carried passively by the current in a river or stream.

ecosystem—a self-supporting unit of interacting organisms and their environment.

ephemeral stream—a stream that flows only during heavy rains.

erosion—the wearing-away of the Earth's surface by water, wind, ice, and other natural forces.

evaporation—the process by which a liquid becomes a gas.

exoskeleton—a rigid external body covering found in certain animals such as insects.

flash flood—a sudden destructive rush of water in a stream or river channel after a storm, resulting from the inability of the soil to absorb the excess water.

food chain—a group of living organisms linked by their feeding relationships.

food web—a network of living organisms linked by their feeding relationships.

gravity—force that pulls objects on the Earth toward the Earth's center.

headwaters—the sources or upper parts of a river.

hectare—a metric unit of measure of area equivalent to 2.471 acres.

hydrograph—a graph of a storm showing stream or river discharge versus time.

hyphae—the filaments that comprise the body of a fungus.

Imhoff cone—a clear cone that holds 1 liter of liquid, used to measure settleable solids in sewage treatment.

index contour lines—heavy brown contour lines on topographic maps.

intermittent stream—a stream channel that carries water during the wet season.

invertebrate—an animal without a backbone.

larva—(plural, *larvae*), an active immature stage in an animal's life history.

macrophytes—plants large enough to be visible without the aid of a magnifying lens.

metamorphosis—a series of changes in the form of an organism as it matures.

molt—process by which some animals shed their outer covering.

nonpoint-source pollutant—a type of pollutant, such as acid rain, that affects part or all of a watershed and the streams and river the watershed feeds.

nymph—a type of larva that resembles the adult animal, typical of such insects as dragonflies.

perennial stream—a body of running water whose sources might be a spring, stormwater, or ground water.

periphyton—minute aquatic organisms, mostly algae and bacteria, that grow on hard surfaces in water.

permeable—a material that allows certain substances to pass through it.

perpendicular—two lines that meet at a right or 90° angle.

petiole—the stalk by which a leaf is attached to the stem.

pH—a measure of the relative acidity, or concentration of hydrogen ions, of a substance. It is rated on a scale of 1 to 14, where 1 is most acidic and 14 is least acidic.

plankton—small aquatic organisms that drift passively in a body of water.

point source pollutant—a pollutant that enters a body of water from a single source such as a pipe.

precipitation—water in the form of rain, snow, hail, or sleet.

producers—living organisms such as plants that are able to use inorganic materials to make their own food.

protists—large group of one-celled organisms including algae and protozoans.

protozoans—minute, mostly microscopic organisms found in marine, freshwater, and moist terrestrial habitats.

pupa—(plural, *pupae*), a seemingly inactive stage in the life of certain insects, during which the larva transforms into an adult.

riffle—a shallow area of a stream characterized by rapid flow, a ripply surface, and a gravel bed.

riparian zone—the area of land and vegetation bordering a stream or river.

run—an area of fast-flowing, deep water in a river or stream.

Secchi disk—a black-and-white disk held by a calibrated line, used by scientists to measure the clarity of standing or running water.

sediment—loose soil resulting from erosion, carried by a stream or river, and deposited in areas of slower flow, creating sandbars, floodplains, and deltas.

seine—large flat net.

silt—fine sediment smaller than sand.

source—water flow that forms the beginning of a stream; may include a glacier, snowfield, spring, marsh, lake, pond, or swamp.

species—(singular or plural), a kind of living organism

whose members breed naturally only with one another and resemble one another more closely than they resemble members of any similar group.

stream order—a system of classifying streams and rivers based on their relationship or position in the drainage network.

substrate—the material that forms the bottom of a stream or any hard surface that stream creatures attach to.

topographic map—a map that shows the features of an area of land, including the shape of the Earth's surface.

transect—in mapping, a line that runs from a baseline, along which distances to various features of the landscape are measured.

tributary—a small stream that flows into a larger stream or river.

vertebrate—an animal with a backbone.

watershed—the land drained by a river or stream and all of its tributaries.

For Further Information

AFTMA's Pocket Guide to Fishing Rivers and Streams. Phoenix, MD: FIM Publishing, Inc., 1989.

Francis, N. and S. Butcher. *Mississippi Madness. Canoeing the Mississippi-Missouri.* Oxford, England: The Oxford Illustrated Press, 1990.

Kellogg, L.L. *Monitor's Guide to Aquatic Macroinvertebrates.* 2nd ed. Gaithersburg, MD: Izaak Walton League of America, 1994.

Lewis, B.A. *The Kid's Guide to Social Action: How to Solve the Social Problems You Choose—And Turn Creative Thinking Into Positive Action.* Minneapolis, MN: Free Spirit Publishing, Inc., 1991.

McCafferty, W.P. *Aquatic Entomology: The Fishermen's and Ecologists' Illustrated Guide to Insects and Their Relatives.* Boston: Science Books International, 1981.

Merritt, R.W. and K.W. Cummins, ed. *An Introduction to the Aquatic Insects of North America.* Dubuque, IA: Kendall/Hunt Publishing Company, 1984.

Murdoch, T., M. Cheo, and K. O'Laughlin. *Streamkeeper's Field Guide. Watershed Inventory and Stream Monitoring Methods.* Everett, WA: Adopt-A-Stream Foundation, 1996.

Needham, J.G. and P.R. Needham. *A Guide to the Study of Freshwater Biology.* 5th ed. San Francisco: Holden-Day, Inc., 1962.

Page, L.M. and B.M. Burr. *A Field Guide to the Freshwater*

Fishes: North America North of Mexico. Boston: Houghton Mifflin Co., 1991.

Petralia, J.F. *Gold! Gold! Beginner's Handbook: How to Prospect for Gold!* San Francisco: Sierra Outdoor Products, 1991.

Prescott, G.W. *How to Know the Freshwater Algae.* Dubuque, IA: Wm. C. Brown Company Publishers, 1970.

Rainis, Kenneth G. and Bruce J. Russell. *Guide to Microlife.* Danbury, CT: Franklin Watts, 1997.

Reid, G.K. *Pond Life. A Guide to Common Plants and Animals of North American Ponds and Lakes.* New York: Golden Press, 1987.

Films and Videos

Restoring America's Streams. Izaak Walton League of America, Save Our Streams Program, 707 Conservation Lane, Gaithersburg, MD 20878-2983.

SOS for America's Streams. Izaak Walton League of America, Save Our Streams Program, 707 Conservation Lane, Gaithersburg, MD 20878-2983.

The Streamkeeper. The Adopt-A-Stream Foundation, 600 128th St. SE, Everett, WA 98208.

Agencies and Organizations

Adopt-A-Stream Foundation
600 128th Street SE,
Everett, WA 98208

American Society of Limnology and Oceanography
5400 Bosque Boulevard, Suite 680
Waco, TX 76710-4446

American Water Works Association
Public Information Department
6666 West Quincy Ave.
Denver, CO 80235

Global Rivers Environmental Education Network
(GREEN)
721 East Huron St.
Ann Arbor, MI 48104

Izaak Walton League of America
707 Conservation Lane
Gaithersburg, MD 20878-2983;

United States Environmental Protection Agency (EPA)
Water Resources Center
401 M St. SW, Washington, DC 20460
Volunteer Monitoring Coordinator: Alice Mayio.

Equipment Suppliers

Carolina Biological Supply Company
2700 York Rd.
Burlington, NC 27215-3398
(800)334-5551
Live water striders can be purchased from March through November.

Forestry Suppliers, Inc.
P.O. Box 8397
Jackson, MS 39284-8397
(800)647-5368
They offer an inexpensive gold-panning kit and miner's pan.

LaMotte Company
P.O. Box 329
Chestertown, MD 21620
(800)344-3100
This company specializes in equipment and test kits for the analysis of water, soil, and air.

Ward's
P.O. Box 92912
Rochester, NY 14692-9012
(800)962-2660
A scientific-supply company that offers an inexpensive Imhoff cone.

Wildlife Supply Company
301 Cass St.
Saginaw, MI 48602
(800)799-8301
Specializes in aquatic sampling instruments and equipment.

United States Geological Survey (USGS)
Information Services
P.O. Box 25286
Denver Federal Center
Denver, CO 80255
(800)435-7627
You can obtain topographic maps for the United States or Puerto Rico. Ask for USGS's free index for any state. Watershed maps or hydrologic unit maps are also available from the USGS. Call (800)426-9000.

Internet Resources
American Society of Limnology and Oceanography
http://aslo.org

Izaak Walton League of America
http://www.iwla.org/

Natural Resources Conservation Service
http://www.nrcs.usda.gov/

North American Benthological Society
http://www.benthos.org

United States Environmental Protection Agency (EPA)
"Surf Your Watershed"
http://www.epa.gov/surf

United States Fish and Wildlife Service
http://www.fws.gov/

United States Geological Survey
   Water Resources Information
   http://h2o.usgs.gov/

   Surface water data retrieval
   http://h2o.usgs.gov/swr
   http://h2o.er.usgs.gov/public/realtime.html

Here are a few of the home pages of school groups doing stream monitoring:
Menomonee River Studies
http://muhs.edu/pages/riverstudies/index.html

Monitoring Little Falls Stream
http://www.mcps.k12.md.us/schools/westbrookes/littlefallsstory.html

Salt Creek Investigation
http://www.ncrel.org/mands/FERMI/saltcreek/stu1.html

Thornton Creek Project
http://h20.lakeside.sea.wa.us/thornton/learning/resource.html

Index